LET'S PLAN AN ASSEMBLY

More assembly topics for 5-8s

ANNE FARNCOMBE

NATIONAL CHRISTIAN EDUCATION COUNCIL

Robert Denholm House
Nutfield, Redhill, Surrey, RH1 4HW

To JOHN, with love

Other books in this series

IT'S OUR ASSEMBLY
Assembly topics for 5-8s

OUR TURN FOR ASSEMBLY
More assembly topics for 5-8s

TIME FOR ASSEMBLY
Assembly topics for 8-12s

(All by Anne Farncombe)

ASSEMBLIES FOR 8-12s

(by Anthony Greenslade
and Herbert Cooke)

First published 1985
© Anne Farncombe

ISBN 0-7197-0436-7

Typeset by Avonset, Midsomer Norton, Bath
Printed in Great Britain at the
University Press, Cambridge

Contents

Introduction

This book is the third in a series published for the 5-8 age group in response to a need expressed by many teachers for material for Assemblies and, in particular, material which is linked to class-room projects.

All the necessary material for Assemblies is provided here including stories, poems, prayers, and suggestions for hymns and music, based on a variety of topics following through the terms of the school year.

The topics are written in outline form, and give sufficient indication of the way in which the projects can be set up in the class-room; the resultant work of the children can be used in various ways at the following Assembly.

The items included for the Assembly are not necessarily listed in the order in which they should be used, and it is hoped that teachers will involve the children in planning which items to include in each Assembly and the order in which they are presented.

Throughout the book, the words Infant school have been used to indicate both Infant and First schools; this is for ease of presentation only. The hymns and songs have been selected from two books: *New Child Songs* (NCEC) and *Someone's Singing, Lord* (A & C Black), both commonly used in Infant and First schools.

Where a suggestion for music is made, an indication is also given of why the piece is recommended, and its particular relationship to the subject of the Assembly. Where no suggestion is made, it was felt that the subject did not readily suggest particular music.

Anne Farncombe is a trained teacher with many years' experience in various schools. She is married to a Chief Inspector of the NSPCC.

Harvest—growing things

Project outline

The aim of the project and the Assembly is to help the children understand that while God provides the soil, the sun, the rain and the plants, it is people who have to work with him to produce the food to eat. Whilst in primitive countries many people still live by hunting and by eating fruit, berries and vegetable matter which has not been cultivated, we are concerned here with those who deliberately prepare the ground, and sow and reap the food by which we live.

These suggestions are for class activities that will not take very long. Divide the class into groups with a 'gardener' or 'farmer' in charge of each group. He or she should not do all the work but should see that the care of the plants, watering, turning to the sunlight, keeping records, etc, is carried out each day by members of the group. It is important that in each activity a 'spare' pot or jar is prepared. Keep it with the others, but give it no further attention. This will help to show that man must assist in the cultivation of God's world.

Group 1 Each child should prepare a margarine (or similar) plastic pot by making a few holes in the base, for drainage, and then filling it with fine soil. (This preparation is an important part of the activity. No farmer or grower would sow seeds without some preparation of the ground.) Sprinkle half a teaspoonful of birdseed over the soil and cover thinly. Small plants will begin to grow in a day or two. Keep them damp but not over-watered. When grown, some of the plants may be identified.

Group 2 Each child will need a jam jar, preferably a large one, and enough mung beans or mixed salad sprouts for about a teaspoonful for each jar. Put the beans into the jar and tie a muslin cover firmly over the opening. Pour warm water through the muslin to fill the jar, shake the beans in it, then pour out the water. Lay the jam jar on its side on a large dish or on some cloth in a warm place. After two days it may be moved to the sunlight. The jam jar should be rinsed with warm water twice a day so that water adheres to the beans most of the time. Point out that at first the seeds or beans are feeding on themselves, but then begin to make their own food by receiving light and moisture. In less than a week the bean shoots can be eaten raw in a salad.

5

Group 3   This group grows mustard seeds on blotting-paper or cotton wool on a saucer. Soak the blotting-paper or cotton wool in water, then keep it damp by laying it on the saucer which is kept 'topped up' with daily watering. Sprinkle the mustard seeds on the surface, and watch them sprout and grow.

Group 4   Jam jars are needed again, blotting-paper, and some ordinary beans (eg, runner beans). Line the jar with soaked blotting-paper and leave enough water in the bottom of the jar to reach the lower edge of the blotting-paper. Push a bean between the blotting-paper and the side of the jar, about half-way down. The bean will soon crack and begin to send out roots, followed by the shoots.

There should be something from most of the groups to show after one week, but if you can begin the experiments, particularly in Groups 1 and 4, about ten days before the Assembly, the results will be more dramatic. The children could show their plants and talk about them, along with any daily records that have been kept. The 'spare' pots or jam jars with their 'uncultivated' plants should be shown and discussed, and the point made about neglect.

The Assembly

Hymns and songs

Ears of corn are waving	NCS 22
We plough the fields, and scatter	NCS 93
Look for signs that summer's done	SSL 54
When the corn is planted	SSL 55
The farmer comes to scatter the seed	SSL 56

Poem (This could be recited by two children, or by two groups of children.)

1st child   Here is a little seed,
        brown and cold and dry;
    what do you want of me,
        seed, so you'll grow by and by?

2nd child   I want a little bed,
        warm and damp and fine,
    where I can lie and sleep,
        then grow, in my own good time.

Then when I start to grow
    long and sturdy roots,
I need the sunshine bright
    for my first green leafy shoots.

Give me some water, too,
    fresh as it can be,
then I shall spread my leaves,
    and you will be proud of me.

1st child   Sleep, little tiny seed,
        'till you stir and grow;
      I will look after your needs,
        and God will help me, I know.

Music
   An Outdoor Overture, Aaron Copland (atmosphere music)

Prayer
   Thank you, Lord God, for the people who look after the land, so that it is ready to grow our food.
   Thank you for the care they take to water the plants and to feed them so that they will grow well.
   Thank you for those who harvest the crops, for those who make food from them, and for those who sell us the food.
   Help us to look for ways of helping you on this earth.

Stories
   Bible stories: The sower—Mark 4.3-8
                  The growing seed—Mark 4.26-29
   The harvest garden (told in full)

The harvest garden

Long before the summer had really started, Mr and Mrs Palmer were thinking about the autumn. They called the children together after tea one day.

'I've had an idea,' said Mr Palmer, and Mrs Palmer nodded to show that she was already in on the secret. Della and Gavin wanted to know what it was immediately, but Ian was still eating the last of the apple pie.

'Come on, Ian,' said Mr Palmer impatiently. 'You're only interested in what goes into your mouth!' He wanted everyone listening at the same time, because he wanted everyone to help in what he was going to suggest. 'Well,' he said, when

Ian had put his plate in the kitchen, 'I was thinking about the Harvest Festival at the church.'

'That's not until September or October!' said Gavin, who knew all about the months of the year.

'I know,' Dad replied, 'but if we left it until then to begin my plan, it would be too late. You know the place in the garden where Ian used to have his rubber play pool—by the garden seat?'

Ian had spent most of the summer in that paddling pool when he was a little boy, two years ago. Sometimes he wished he hadn't grown too big for it.

'I thought perhaps we could clear that patch of garden,' Dad went on, 'and you three could use it specially to grow things for the Harvest Festival.'

'It's a marvellous idea,' said Mother. 'You could each have a piece of garden and grow something. It would be your very own, and you could take what you grow there to the church later on.'

Della, Gavin and Ian thought it was a good idea too, and started to talk about what they would grow.

'A pear-tree!' said Ian, who was very fond of pears.

'Don't be silly!' Gavin said. 'It would take years and years to grow a pear-tree. I think I'll plant carrots and beetroot in my bit.'

'Perhaps I could put in some runner beans,' said Della, 'and some cabbages.'

'Tomatoes!' said Ian suddenly. 'Can I grow tomatoes?' He loved eating tomatoes, sinking his teeth into the skin and squirting juice everywhere. Mum said this wasn't the proper way to eat tomatoes, but it was jolly good fun!

Next day, Ian wanted to rush out and buy his tomato plants.

'Wait!' said Dad. 'You haven't got your patch of earth ready yet. Here's a fork; get digging!'

They all worked hard on the bit of garden, and when it was all brown and ready, with no weeds or stones in it at all, Dad divided it into three portions, one for Della, one for Gavin, and one for Ian. He stretched string across and tied it to pegs in the ground, to show where each patch finished.

'Now,' said Dad, 'I'll give you some money each so that you can buy seeds or plants. After that, it's up to you!'

'And God,' said Della.

'You're right,' said Dad, 'but God doesn't do all the work. He needs your help.'

Next day Dad took them to a place where they could buy seeds and plants. Gavin bought a packet of beetroot seeds, and a packet of carrot seeds. That didn't use up all his money, so he bought a small watering-can as well. Della spent her money on a box of young green beans. There were about twelve in the box, and they were beginning to grow into healthy young plants. Dad said he would show her how to put sticks in her bit of garden for the bean plants to grow up. She had just enough money left to buy four cabbage plants, and Dad said that was all she'd have room for by the time she'd put all her beans in the ground. Ian chose three tomato plants and a blackberry bush.

'But you won't get fruit from that by September!' said Mother, when he showed the blackberry bush to her later. Ian was disappointed, and hoped that she was wrong.

The seeds and plants were put into the beds immediately; what a good thing they had prepared the ground well! Soon little green shoots showed up in rows where Gavin had planted his beetroot and carrot seeds, and he watered them each day when there was no rain. Dad and Della had made a sort of skeleton wigwam out of long sticks tied together at the top, and Della had planted a bean plant by the bottom of each stick. It wasn't long before most of them grew tall enough to start climbing up round the sticks. Della pretended they were having a race to see who could reach the top first. Her four cabbages were planted not far away.

Ian dug nice deep holes for his tomatoes, so that their roots could have lots of room. Dad showed him how to put a stick beside each one, and how to tie the plants gently to it, so that they wouldn't be blown over by a strong wind or in a rainstorm. Ian was cross when Dad said his blackberry bush would need cutting down as soon as it was planted. 'Then it will grow more strongly,' said Dad.

June and July went past quite quickly. On most days the sun was bright and hot, and on others the rain came down. 'Just the sort of weather gardeners like,' said Gavin, who felt as if he'd been a gardener all his life. His seeds had grown into healthy plants, although there were too many of them close together. Dad advised him to pull out some of the smaller ones, so that the larger ones would have more room to grow. Of course the carrots themselves, and the beetroot, were hidden under the earth, but the leaves on the top looked good and healthy.

Della's beans had climbed right to the top of the long sticks, and the skeleton wigwam now looked like a big green tent of leaves, and there were lots of little red flowers to be seen. The bees visited them every day. Dad said that soon there would be beans for her to pick.

The tomato plants that Ian had put in had grown fast, and as the yellow flowers dropped their petals they left behind tiny green tomatoes. In the third week of July one of them had got very big, and had turned red in the sun.

'There's a tomato, a big red tomato in my garden!' Ian cried, rushing indoors one day. The others went to look, and admired it. Ian was waiting for Dad when he came home from work. 'I had a great big red tomato on my plant!' he called as Dad drove the car into the garage at five o'clock. 'I'll come and look,' said Dad.

'No, you can't!' said Ian. 'I've eaten it!'

Dad sighed, but he wasn't surprised. Ian did like food so much!

As August went by, Della picked her beans, and Mother froze packets of them, cut up ready for eating. 'You can take these to the Harvest Festival,' she told Della. 'They will be lovely for the old people to eat.'

'My carrots and beetroot will be big enough to pull up just before harvest,' Gavin announced proudly.

Ian ate so many of his tomatoes as they ripened that Mother couldn't even make them into tomato sauce for him to take to the church.

On Harvest Festival Sunday, Gavin carried a box full of newly dug carrots and beetroot. He had cleaned every one in the kitchen sink, and they looked bright and fresh. Della took a basket full of beans she had picked the night before, and, in a cold bag, lots of small packets that had been frozen. Two of her cabbages had grown big, too, so she took them along.

Ian looked at his tomato plants. They were going yellow; there were only two little tomatoes left, and they were hard and green.

'Oh dear,' said Mother.

'Whatever happened?' said Dad, who knew exactly what had happened to them.

Ian had nothing he had grown to take to the Harvest service. He looked very miserable, but Father knew how to cheer him up. He took Ian to one side and whispered in his ear. 'Next year you could have as much as Gavin and Della have this year,' he said. 'Look after that blackberry plant. It's already putting out long shoots that will have blackberries on next year. There'll be lots of fruit, and it will all be ripe just about at harvest time! But it won't be for you; you must grow them for other people. Promise?'

Ian smiled, and promised. So his blackberry bush was a good idea after all. He was sure of having something for the Harvest Festival next year. He began to plan how to take care of the new long shoots over the winter months. He smiled a secret smile in church that morning as the minister read:

'As long as the world exists, there will be a time for planting and a time for harvest. There will always be cold and heat, summer and winter, day and night.'   (Genesis 8.22, GNB)

Acquisitiveness

Project outline

One of the maladies of today's world is the importance and value attached to material possessions. Homes must have the latest domestic aids; technological equipment has become prized in the office and on the shop floor; and computers, calculators and videos are no longer the toys of the rich. Children are offered ever bigger and better playthings. We cannot really blame the children who brag about the things they have, nor silence those who whine for something they have not got, when most of them are witnesses to this sort of acquisitiveness from the cradle on.

When we compare our own *wants* with the *needs* of the Thirld World, we ought to feel ashamed—and some do. But unfortunately even this awareness rarely changes attitudes for long. It may stir us to make donations or speeches, but few of us would be willing to deny ourselves, or our children, the new TV set, or the holiday, or the extension needed for the house.

How can we expect our children to appreciate the necessary things with which we are blessed—enough food to eat, homes, clothing to wear, and a free country in which to live? How can we show them that these things in themselves make them rich and privileged, whatever their next-door neighbour possesses?

The aim of this project will be to help the children recognise the difference between 'wanting' and 'needing'.

Food Without the right kind of food we would waste and die. List all the food the children were given to eat yesterday; talk about milk and how necessary it is for babies; and bread, how much is bought and consumed by families every week; talk about the value of fresh fruit and vegetables.

Then contrast this with the amount of food available for the underfed children in other countries. Refer to countries in the news because of famine or other disaster causing near-starvation.

Water In a similar way, stress the value of water and rainfall, for washing, for cooking, for the growing of crops, etc, and then point out that in many countries children fall ill and die when rain does not come.

Clothing Pursue the same line with the clothes we wear; compare what we wear in cold weather with what is needed in hot weather. Contrast this with the

11

rags and third- or fourth-hand torn clothing possessed by the underprivileged, where the sparseness of clothing often has little to do with the heat of the sun.

Homes Invite the children to draw or describe the homes they live in, not forgetting the 'luxuries' of a TV set, washing-machine, refrigerator, etc. However poor, they have the certainty of a roof, four walls, and a place to go home to, whereas many children live in shanty towns and ghettoes, or as refugees, in filth and misery.

A free country For young children this is too complex a subject to tackle at length. Suffice it to remind them that any of them, even those of other religions, are free to browse round a church, or attend services if they wish. In many countries this is a freedom that is denied to Christians, let alone others, and this needs to be stated, however simply.

So these things go to make up our *needs*; you may be able to add others. It will be necessary to go on to discuss with the children some of the things they *want*, like new toys, games, clothes, etc. Examine each one and try to establish whether what is desired is needed or simply wanted.

At the Assembly, try to do two things:

> contrast what we, in this country, can enjoy that is denied to many other children in the world;
>
> bring out the difference between wanting and needing.

The Assembly

Hymns and Songs

'Click' goes the switch	NCS 33
The sun that shines acrosss the sea	SSL 11
O Jesus, we are well and strong	SSL 40

Poem

Living together

Sometimes I feel the sunshine,
　　sometimes I hear the rain;
I see the stars come out at night,
　　and watch the moon again.
Around the world are boys and girls
　　who see the same bright sun,
who watch the big white moon rise up
　　when all the daylight's gone.

12

We walk upon the same round earth,
   those boys and girls and I;
we breathe the air, we feel the wind,
   and see the clouds so high;
but when I think of all I have,
   I wish that they, like me,
could have the things I value most—
   like breakfast, dinner, tea.

I cannot send my food to them,
   I cannot hold their hands,
but I can pray for them, and know
   God holds them in *his* hands.
Perhaps one day, when I am grown,
   people will learn to care
as much for them as for themselves;
   that they will learn to share.

Prayer
   For our food and homes and toys,
      thank you, Father God.
   There are many girls and boys,
      bless them, Father God,
   who would like to share our bread,
      love them, Father God;
   for them now our prayers are said,
      hear them, Father God.

Stories
   Bible story: The rich man—Mark 10.17-22
   What Nigel wanted (told in full)

What Nigel wanted

Nigel was seven, and was looking forward to the best holiday of his life. Auntie Val and Uncle Baz, who had a farm near Bristol, had invited him to stay; not only that, but they had said that he and his cousin Barry could have a tent, and camp in the farm garden!

'Let's hope it doesn't rain,' said Grandma, who always thought that rain mattered. 'You'll come home with a cold if you get wet!'

Of course I won't, said Nigel to himself, and thought how nice it would be to crawl into a little tent and hear the rain beating down all round.

He told his friends at school about his coming holiday.

'I went camping,' said Robert. 'You'll need a torch!'

'And a compass,' added Charles, whose father had explored a jungle. Nigel couldn't think why he'd need a compass in the farm garden, but it would be fun to have one.

'I hope your wellington boots are strong enough,' said Grandma later, 'and you ought to have a waterproof watch. When your father went camping about twenty years ago he fell in the river. His waterproof watch kept going all the time!'

Nigel didn't intend going too near a river; he did not like water much, and he could not swim well. But a waterproof watch! He could wear it in the bath!

He had a card from Barry, his cousin. 'Bring a penknife,' it said. 'Then we can hack our way through the hedge and explore the cows' field.'

Nigel showed the card to his mother. 'Hack through the hedge?' she said. 'Uncle Baz will have something to say if you do that! What's the matter with the gate? Besides, knives are dangerous. You might cut yourself.'

Nigel counted his saved-up pocket-money, then made a list of all the things he wanted to buy before they got to the farm. Mum and Dad and Grandma were all going to take him, in the car, and Dad said they must arrive about tea-time. 'Then you can set up the tent long before it gets dark,' he said.

It was quite a long way from Shrewsbury to Bristol, but Dad knew the way well. 'We'll have lunch in Worcester,' he promised, 'and you can do your shopping after that. It'll make a good break in the journey.'

It was not very comfortable in the car. Dad had put Nigel's luggage in the boot, but there were his wellington boots and a new sleeping-bag squashed in between Nigel and Grandma on the back seat. And Mum had insisted that their dog, Biscuit, should come as well, so that he could enjoy a good run at the farm when they arrived. Biscuit was not very good at sitting still in the car. He panted, and licked the windows, and threw himself all over Nigel, and left hairs on the new sleeping-bag. And Nigel began to feel car sick. He was glad when at last they reached Worcester, but Dad spent such a long time finding a place to park the car that it was nearly two o'clock when they walked into a cafe for lunch.

'We'll have to leave Worcester by 3.30,' warned Dad. 'Even if we go all the way to Bristol on the motorway, we shan't get there before five o'clock, then we've got to get out to the farm at Dundry. And we said we'd be there for tea!'

Mum hurried Nigel through his fish and chips. 'Come on,' she said. 'Let's get your shopping, Nigel. Where's your list?'

Grandma went back to the car to keep Biscuit company, while Dad went to browse round the cathedral. Nigel counted his money again. Mum said he must buy the things he *wanted* with that, as she had bought him the things he *needed*. Nigel found it difficult to know what the difference was, but he knew the sleeping-bag had cost more than Mum thought it would, so she was a bit short of money.

'But I *need* a torch, and a compass, and a waterproof watch,' Nigel pointed out. He wasn't going to mention the penknife he also needed. If he saw one, he would just buy it, and tell Mum later on.

'I agree a torch would be useful,' said Mother, 'but what you want a compass and a waterproof watch for I can't imagine. But hurry up, do. Dad will be really cross if we're not back in time.'

They found a chemist. Mum said they could buy a torch in there.

'But I want a camping torch!' protested Nigel, dragging Mum to a shop that sold things like tents and climbing boots.

The torches there were rather special rubber ones, very large and expensive.

14

Perhaps torches at the chemist would cost less. Nigel spotted a plastic mug. 'I want one of those!' he said, choosing a red one and counting out some of his money.

They had to walk some way back to the chemist. 'That's what I want!' said Nigel, pointing to a torch which was big and had three different coloured lights— red, green and yellow. It was rather expensive, and Mum said he ought to buy a cheaper one, but Nigel thought red, green and yellow lights might be useful for signalling to the cows in the middle of the night, so he bought it. The batteries were not included in the price, but Mother said she would buy those for him.

'Now we'll go to Woolworths and get my compass,' said Nigel, pulling Mother along the main shopping street. Woolworths was right at the end, and it was packed. Nigel couldn't find a compass anywhere.

'Come back to the car-park now,' said Mother. 'It's getting late.'

'One minute, there were some compasses in that camping shop,' said Nigel. 'I must have a compass!'

Mother trailed behind while Nigel rushed to the camping shop. The cheapest compass was £2, and it did not look very strong. Nigel looked at the penknives instead.

'I want a penknife,' he said to the assistant.

'Double-bladed, or one with ten different blades?' asked the man.

'I'll look at them all!' said Nigel.

Mother, who was standing by the door looking at her watch, was trying to hurry him. As the shop assistant spread five knives on the counter, she came over quickly. 'Nigel,' she said, 'it's nearly quarter to four! Dad will be getting very impatient. Come on!'

Nigel looked at the knives; Mother hadn't really noticed what he was trying to buy. He knew he would have to go, but he also knew he wanted one of those knives. 'How much is this one?' he asked.

'Well, that one has five blades,' said the assistant. 'It's £7.'

Nigel gasped. 'I'll have that one,' he said, pointing to a single-bladed small knife.

The assistant told him how much the knife cost. Nigel counted his money slowly and carefully. He was 30p short.

'Nigel!' Mother was shouting.

The man at the counter looked round at her. Nigel wanted to slip one of the knives into his pocket while the assistant's head was turned. He *must* have one. The man looked back, before Nigel could do anything. Nigel felt quite glad, because he knew that it would have been stealing, and he did not really want to steal.

'Can I pay 30p less?' he asked.

'Sorry, son,' said the assistant. 'You must pay the full price.'

Nigel shook his head sadly. Perhaps Mother would give him the rest of the money. Perhaps she wouldn't, though, not for a knife. Besides, she had gone out of the shop door to ask the way back to the car-park. Nigel left the shop quickly, with no penknife. Mother had disappeared! He decided she must have gone back to the car-park without him. He knew the way.

He *thought* he knew the way. It seemed further than he imagined. He walked past the cathedral and out through the gardens beyond. Then he turned up a little street, beginning to run. He did not know where he was. He was not going to cry. Boys who went camping did not cry, but his eyes watered, and he rubbed them dry on his sleeve. Bump! Nigel had run straight into a policeman!

'What's up, lad?' asked the policeman.

'I can't find the car-park,' said Nigel.

'Do you know which one?' Nigel shook his head. 'Well, we'll try this one first,' said the policeman. 'Come with me.'

The first person they saw was Mum, at the car-park entrance. 'Where did you get to?' she asked, sounding very cross, as the policeman handed Nigel over. 'I went into the shop three times and you weren't there. I was only just outside!' Nigel must have missed her somehow.

'It's half past four!' said Dad, storming up. 'Get in the car.'

They drove in silence. It was quicker on the motorway, but they did not get to the farm until half past six. Auntie Val was getting worried and his cousin Barry was annoyed.

'By the time we've had tea, and Dad's done the milking, it'll be too late to put the tent up before dark. Mum says we'll have to do it tomorrow now.'

Nigel was terribly disappointed. It would not be nearly so much fun to sleep in a proper bed, looking at a proper ceiling!

'Whatever made you so late?' asked Uncle Baz. Mum and Dad and Grandma looked at Nigel.

'I wanted too much,' said Nigel, sadly. He wished he had not spent all that time *wanting* things, especially things he did not really *need*. He knew the difference now.

Disappointment

Project outline

Those teachers who are also mothers will know that disappointments for our children are among the hardest things for us to bear. Somehow we cope with times when the children are in pain, or are bullied, when they are sad or frightened. But we feel so helpless when confronted by their disappointments. It seems uselessly inadequate to tell them that life is full of disappointments, that they have only just begun to experience them, and will become used to them as they grow older. Do we ever become quite adjusted to disappointment? Perhaps some of us feel disappointment just as keenly now as we did when we were children.

Nevertheless, we can teach our children that disappointments are very rarely 'the end'; that often out of them, or because of them, we can find new opportunities and new openings, and we can always learn a little more about ourselves or other people.

Little project work is suggested. A class or an individual disappointment may be all you need to lead into the worship. You may be able to find other stories and poems which illustrate the theme; if so, tell them or read them during the week leading up to your Assembly. The children might write or draw about times when they have felt let down, when what they wanted to have, or do, did not appear, or happen. Ask about how they felt at the time, and about anything that has happened since to make them feel better. Some children may like to draw their own faces to show their expressions of disappointment. These pictures could be shown, and any written work read and talked about, during the Assembly.

The Assembly

Hymns and songs

When we are happy, full of fun	NCS 29
Father, we thank you for the night	NCS 32, SSL 1
When I needed a neighbour	SSL 35
Look out for loneliness	SSL 36

Poem

The Bad Day

I'm cross and fed up,
I'm awfully sad,
something has happened
to make me feel bad.

      I wanted to go to the zoo today
      and Mummy had promised that I could play
      on the see-saws and swings,
      and roundabouts too,
      which everyone knows
      are there at the zoo.
      I was going to see
      the monkeys and bear,
      the parrot and llama,
      and when we got there
      I could have an ice cream,
      potato crisps too;
      it was going to be lovely,
      my day at the zoo.

But when I woke up
it was pouring with rain,
and someone had altered
the time of the train.
Mum had a headache,
and I had a sneeze,
so the outing was cancelled;
and now, if you please,
the zoo's closed for winter—
not open till spring,
and nothing will make
me smile, not a thing!

Prayer

Most of the time we feel happy, O God, but there are days when we feel really
sad and miserable. Please help us to smile and be glad when other people seem
to have all the fun, or all the luck. We know that we have you for a friend, and
that you love us all the time.

18

   Bible story: The disappointed disciples (to be simplified)—Luke 24.13-32
   Julie's song (told in full)

Julie's song

Julie Philips had a lovely voice. Grandma said she could sing like a bird, and
Grandpa said she ought to go on television. Julie sang all the time: when she woke
up in the morning, when she walked with Mummy and Baby Ben to school, when
she went into the sweet-shop, and when she was in the bath at night. Oh yes, she
had a lovely voice, and she could keep in tune.

One day the head teacher at her school told all the boys and girls that the autumn
term music competition would be held soon, and that anyone could go in for it.
There was a competition for those who were learning the piano, for those who
could play the recorder, and for those who could sing. There were special class
competitions, too, for the best percussion band, and the best choir; and all the
parents and grandparents, all the brothers and sisters and aunts and uncles, and all
the friends and neighbours, could come and listen. Every child had a letter to take
home about it.

'You must sing, Julie,' said Grandma.

'Of course she will,' said Grandpa.

And, 'I'll help you practise,' said Mummy.

Julie was also chosen for her class choir, and she said that she would help in the
percussion band, as long as she could play the bells. Of course, the trouble with
Julie was that she thought she was better than everybody else. She just knew she
would win.

At last the day of the concert came. It was to start at six o'clock, after the boys
and girls had been home for tea. Mum had made Julie a new dress: it was pale
blue and had lace at the neck and all round the frill at the bottom. Grandma
brushed Julie's hair until it shone, and Grandpa polished her shoes.

'You'll win, our Julie,' Grandpa said, as they walked down the road to the
school.

Of course she would; Julie knew that. From her class, her best friend Madeline
was entered for the singing competition, and so was Fiona Grant, Akel Patel, and
Tommy Breeze. Also a new girl called Shani Kalsi who had come from Pakistan.

Julie and the others had to wait in a class-room until it was their turn to sing.
Tommy went first, looking pinker and cleaner than Julie had ever seen him. She
could hear him singing.

'He's squeaky!' she whispered, giggling with Madeline.

Next the teacher called Madeline's name, and she froze. 'I can't,' she said. 'I
can't!'

The teacher coaxed her onto the stage and Madeline sang, but she was so quiet that Julie could hardly hear her. After that Akel went on stage, and then it was Julie's turn. She was singing a song that she knew well, called *In the sunshine*. Her voice was clear, and loud, and she was in tune. When she had finished, every mother, father, grandparent and all their friends and relations clapped loudly. Julie stood there, smiling. Grandpa had taught her how to bow, so she did that, before skipping off the stage.

'I was good, wasn't I?' she said to the teacher. 'I think I'll get the prize!'

'Ssh!' said the teacher. 'Go back into the class-room; it's Fiona's turn now.'

Fiona wasn't very good; Julie could not think why she had entered. She could not reach the high notes and had forgotten the words. Julie put her hands over her ears. When Fiona came back, the new girl, Shani Kalsi, went onto the stage. Julie had never heard her sing before. She had hardly heard her talk, come to that. Shani did not know a lot of English, and no one knew her very well. She always looked a bit frightened, and spent a lot of time by herself. Julie heard her sing. Well, it wasn't a bad voice, she thought. She might even come third or fourth. The audience were clapping rather loudly.

Julie had to wait right until the end of the whole evening's competition to know if she had won the singing. She and the others were shown back to where their parents were sitting. Julie looked round at Madeline and grinned. Shani was sitting at the side of the hall with her mother, who wore a blue sari. Shani was looking a bit frightened still, and had cuddled right up to her mother.

'You were right good, our Julie,' said Grandpa, in a loud whisper. 'You'll win all right!'

Julie smiled proudly, and wondered what the prize would be.

'And now we're going to announce all the winners,' said Mrs Black, the head teacher, when she had told all the boys and girls how good they had been. She began by saying which class had won the percussion band section which had been held first of all. The prize went to one of the top classes. Julie was in a middle class. Never mind, she would win the singing prize.

She clapped loud and long when Mrs Black said that Madeline had won the recorder prize, because Madeline was her very best friend, and she was much better at playing the recorder than she was at singing.

'And now for the singing prize,' announced Mrs Black, and Julie patted her hair down and put on her loveliest smile, so that Mummy and Grandpa and Grandma would be really proud of her when she got up to walk to the front.

'The prize winner is in the middle school,' said Mrs Black. Julie knew that; she was in the middle school. 'This year the prize goes to a girl who has got a really lovely voice. We hope we shall hear more of it later on.'

Julie smiled; she might be asked to sing her song again.

'The winner,' said Mrs Black, 'is Shani Kalsi!'

Julie had been just about to push past everyone else in her row, to go up to the front. For one minute she thought she should still go, for surely Mrs Black had simply muddled up the names! But Mrs Black was looking straight at Shani Kalsi, and not at Julie Philips.

'Come along, Shani,' said Mrs Black again. Shani's mother smiled and whispered something to the dark little girl beside her. Shani crept out of her seat and walked up to the front. Mrs Black gave her a little silver cup. 'Well done, Shani,' she said.

Julie felt as if someone had hit her on the head. She sat in her seat with her mouth open, her smile all gone.

'Never mind, lass,' Grandpa was saying. 'That Indian girl was very good. You can't win them all, you know!'

Julie was furious now. She wanted to stand up and tell everybody that *she* was Julie Philips, and that *she* should have won the prize. Instead, she found herself crying with disappointment.

'Why did Shani have to win?' she shouted at Mother on the way home. 'She's new! And nobody's her friend!'

'Then perhaps winning a prize is just what she needs,' said Mother, sensibly and kindly. 'I'm sure it will help her to settle down at school and make friends. She's awfully scared of the rest of you, you know.'

Julie thought about that when she was tucked up in bed that night. Perhaps she would talk to Shani tomorrow; perhaps she would even play with her; perhaps they could sing together with their good voices. Perhaps . . .

Just as she was falling asleep, Julie realised that she didn't feel cross any more. She had been terribly sad and unhappy, and she still felt a bit disappointed, but that was only how Shani would be feeling now if Julie had won. As Shani was new, and lonely, and frightened, perhaps winning was the best thing that could have happened to her.

Caring for pets

Project outline

The project leading up to the Assembly, and the Assembly itself, should aim at making the children aware that, while it is fun to have pets, these pets are in need of constant, ongoing care. When the novelty of having them has worn off, and they are taken for granted as much as is the furniture in the room, they still need loving care to survive and flourish. In order to recognise ongoing care, we shall look at situations in which people look after others constantly, in the home, institution and school. If you have only a short time in which to work through this project, choose only one of the situations. If you could extend the topic beyond the Assembly it might be possible to look at each of them in more detail.

In hospital If someone in the class has recently been in hospital, is there now, or is to go shortly, this would be an ideal time to look at the care with which doctors, nurses, dieticians, surgeons, kitchen workers, porters and ward orderlies carry on their work. Find out what the children know about hospital life; if this is minimal, perhaps a nurse from the children's ward of the local hospital could come into the class-room to talk about her work, the daily routine of the ward. This routine should include not only doctors and nurses, but all those who go into the ward to help care for the patients' welfare: the cleaners, voluntary workers, and the teachers who visit to educate the long-term patients. Ask the visitor to stress the routine, how the same things go on daily, whatever the mood or personal problems of the people who care.

In an institution In a similar way, invite house-parents from a children's home, or a worker from a handicapped persons' centre or old people's home, to come and talk about their work in constant care for others.

In school Look at the things in school life that are constant from day to day, which give a feeling of security to the children by the very routine of their happening. Older children could keep a detailed diary for a week, noting the times and places of regular occurrences. If you have kitchens, others could visit them and interview the staff, or the cleaners, or the caretaker. The boys and girls could do some imaginative writing about what would happen if the workers were careless in their duties, or if they failed to do them on a regular basis.

In the home   What does Mother do all day? And Father? Make a list of jobs that have to be done in the home each day, those that have to be done about once a week, and those that are necessary only occasionally. Do Mother and Father each have a pattern to their day? Try to find out what it is. What happens when Father or Mother cannot perform their duties? Does someone come in as a substitute (eg, grandparent, neighbour, colleague)? In the home, do grandparents give their love as well as practical help?

In any of the situations examined above, make the point that each person gives ongoing care, day to day, month by month, and year by year. The care does not stop, either, though people may fall ill, or leave. By realising this, the children should learn a little about the constant care they ought to give, however boring and routine, to the people and animals they have and towards which they have a responsibility.

The Assembly

Hymns and songs

In the winter, birds need food	NCS 26
A little tiny bird	SSL 24
I love God's tiny creatures	SSL 42
Little birds in winter time	SSL 43

Poem

Our pets

We've got a hamster
sitting on a nest;
we know what hamsters
   like best.
Give them some dinner,
lots of bedding, hay,
then they will be happy
   all day.

We've got a goldfish
swimming round and round;
he likes his fish food,
   we've found.
Wipe down the glass sides,
keep his water clear,
then he will be happy
   all year.

We've got a gerbil
busy every day;
he's got a big cage
    for play.
Keeping the cage clean
isn't always fun,
but he'll be glad when
    it's done.

Let's not forget them,
pets we see each day,
for if we want them
    to stay,
they need our caring,
we must never rest,
giving them always
    our best.

Prayer

Dear God, we know you love all creatures, and you need our help to look after them. Sometimes we find this messy, or boring, or a nuisance, but if we stop caring for them they will die. We do love them, but we must show that we do by making sure they are clean, comfortable and well fed, because they depend upon us. Help us to look after them gladly, even when we don't feel like it.

Stories

Bible verses: Psalm 136.1-4, 25-26; explain to the children first the meaning of the words 'endures for ever' (NEB) or 'eternal' (GNB)

Anna's kitten (told in full)

Anna's kitten

There was once a tiny, tiny kitten, who woke up one morning to find he was in a very strange place. He was terribly cold, very hungry, and all alone. His fur was damp and sticky, and he opened his mouth to cry. Such a little 'Mew, mew' it was, too. The tiny kitten, whose eyes were only just open, looked round to see where he was. He could see empty tins, wet newspapers, and old rags, and there was a strong smell of rotting food. Can you guess where he was? He was on a rubbish tip, his little paws standing in the dirt, and his black coat speckled with dust and damp with the morning rain.

'Mew, mew!' he cried again.

'What's this?' said a kindly voice, and a big gloved hand appeared overhead, just like a black umbrella.

The tiny kitten felt himself lifted up while the big dustman examined him. 'Here, Joe, look at this!' the dustman called to the driver of the dust-cart which had emptied its load onto the tip. 'Got a box there?' he asked. 'There's a kitten here; I can't leave it, Joe. I'll take it home at lunch-time.'

The box they found for the kitten was a comfort to him. It had tall sides and dry newspaper at the bottom. The tiny kitten lay, too exhausted to cry any more, and slept. When he woke up again, three pairs of eyes were looking into his box.

'It's a kitten, Gladys,' the dustman was saying. 'I found it on the tip this morning.'

'Looks more like a wet rat!' said his wife. 'It's too young to live, Frank. It's shaking with cold and hunger. What are we going to do?'

'I'll get a blanket from my doll's pram,' said a third voice. 'Better still, let's put it in the doll's pram! It'll get nice and warm in there!'

'And I've got a dropper in the kitchen drawer,' said Mrs Dustman. 'I'll heat some milk, and see if the kitten will take it from that.'

It wasn't long before the tiny kitten felt warm and cosy. He hadn't got a mother any longer, but these kind people were doing all they could to keep him alive. The little girl, Anna, had wiped the dusty marks from his fur very gently, and he had swallowed the drops of milk hungrily. Now all he wanted to do was sleep.

A conversation was going on round 'his' doll's pram.

'Can we keep him? Please!' said Anna.

'Oh, I expect he'll fit in somewhere,' said her mother. 'But you must look after him,' she added. 'He'll need milk quite often, so I'll show you exactly how to get it ready and give it to him. We'll have to take him to the vet, too, to get his advice on how to look after him. He'll need all our care, not just today, tomorrow and for several weeks until he gets stronger, but maybe for years after that!'

Anna already loved the kitten. 'He'll be all right,' she said. 'I'll do everything for him, I promise.'

Several months later a sleek black cat sat by the fire in the dustman's house. He licked his fur vainly and his whole body trembled with his loud purring. Anna had been as good as her word: she had fed him, kept him warm, and taught him his manners. Never again had he been cold, or hungry, or unloved, because Anna had cared for him every single day. She was sometimes tired, and sometimes bored with the work, but she had never stopped loving him and looking after him.

Responsibility

Project outline

It is never too early to begin learning about responsibility. Right from their earliest days at school some children can be singled out for tasks or messages, and soon become labelled as responsible and reliable. Others, due to timidity, lack of response, or laziness, may need special 'nursing' to train them along the road to proper responsibility. But every child can be encouraged to realise that each should be responsible to other people; that they are not above and beyond the needs of others, and cannot behave with complete disregard for those around them. The project should first enable them to find out how necessary other people are to their well-being and their comfort, and then to look at ways in which they could respond to this awareness.

Begin with a few simple experiences of finding themselves 'alone'. For set times, only a few moments at first, and then extending during longer periods of the school day, ask them to pretend that each one is alone on an island. They may not talk to other children, touch them, or signal to them. They must find something to do completely alone, without communicating with anyone else, which also includes you, the teacher. Later, draw them together again to talk about what it felt like.

The next stage is to talk to the children about certain tasks that can be done alone, and set some of these for them to do. Get them to remember what they have to do by themselves at home: washing, feeding, dressing, etc. Make a chart, or refer to an existing one, where tasks such as tying shoe-laces, knotting ties, doing up buttons, and so on, are listed and recorded. Then look at things done at school: reading, writing, imaginative writing, number work, etc, where, after initial teaching help, the children work alone, and are encouraged to do so.

Then set up games that are normally played by more than one person, and ask the children to play them alone. These could include *I spy,* board games, noughts and crosses, etc. The children will soon complain that they need someone else to join in, and will find no satisfaction or fun in trying to play the games alone.

Also try singing: ask each child to think secretly of a nursery rhyme. Say, 'When I signal, we shall all begin to sing together.' The result, of course, will be noisy, discordant and meaningless. 'What is wrong?' you ask. Let the children answer, then ask for suggestions for a way of making the 'performance' more pleasing. They will soon realise that if each child contributes the same words and tune the effect will not only be more satisfying, but clear and intelligible. Each child, at this point, has contributed something to the whole and, at the same time, become aware of the contributions of others.

At the next session act out situations where one child has needs which could be met by another, eg, a poor reader might be helped by a reading game played with a more able child; a child who has fallen over could be helped up and taken to an adult for treatment; a child unable to cut with scissors could be given help by one more competent, and so on. In each situation presented, ask the boys and girls what help is needed, and then for their suggestions as to how the need could be met by them. Also stress that those in need do not always ask for help, and that being on the look-out for, or spotting, the need, is as much a part of the responsibility as the actual giving of help.

During the few days immediately before the Assembly, make sure each child in the class is given the opportunity to behave responsibly, in the taking of messages, tidying the room, or helping another child. There will not be much to display at the Assembly, but the children can contribute by talking about the jobs they do, and ways in which they have been able to help others. They could act out the biblical story of ten girls who were given the opportunity to behave responsibly, but who did not all respond (Matthew 25.1-13)

The Assembly

Hymns and songs

Father, we thank you for the night	NCS 32
Hands to work and feet to run	SSL 21
When I needed a neighbour	SSL 35
Think, think on these things	SSL 38

Poem
Things I can do
There are things I can do that are done by one,
like brushing my teeth (which can be quite fun
when I squeeze the tube and the toothpaste goes
               on my nose).

I can eat my lunch by myself, with a fork,
I can dress myself when we go for a walk,
I can read a bit, when school-time comes,
               and do sums.

But it's sometimes best to have two or more—
For playing some games you really need four;
I can't play *I spy* on my own, or get placed
                              in a race.

And when I need help I want somebody there,
like when I fall down, or get knots in my hair,
and when I am ill I want someone to come,
                              like my Mum.

When others are hurt, or unhappy, or sad,
they also need someone to help them be glad;
and sometimes that someone, it's easy to see,
                              could be me.

Prayer
Here are my two hands, Lord;
here are my two feet,
make them always ready,
at home, in school, or street.
And here are my two eyes, Lord,
make them quick to see
where I could be helping
someone who needs me.

Stories
Bible story: The parable of the ten girls—Matthew 25.1-13
Sharing the work (told in full)

Sharing the work

Mother was putting all the food into her new larder. It was only a small cupboard, and David could see that Mother was being very careful to make it tidy. All the tins of food went together on one shelf, all the sauces and pickles on another, and the vegetables were put in a rack on the floor: potatoes on the bottom layer, and carrots and onions on top.

They had only just moved into this house. It was smaller than their previous one. Mother had told David that, because it was smaller, they would need to be tidier, putting things away when they had finished with them, and so on.

David's bedroom was so small that it was difficult to move round the bed. He had a wardrobe, too, and a dressing-table, but there was a little corner by the door where he had a big cardboard box for his toys. If he didn't remember to put away his train, and his bricks, and his cars, there wasn't room to get undressed at night, and certainly no room for his mother to sit anywhere when she came to read him a story before he went to sleep.

For a few weeks David was very careful, but then the cold weather came and he had to bring his toys downstairs and play with them in the warm living-room. Sometimes he brought down so many that it was difficult to carry them all up again, and he began to be careless.

'You left your ball downstairs again,' Mother would say, bringing it up with her when he was in bed. Sometimes she said, 'Go back, David, you've forgotten your books,' and David would have to climb out of his cosy bed to clear them up.

One winter evening when he got home from school his shoes were wet and muddy. 'I'll clean them!' David said, knowing Mother would be pleased that she did not have to do it for him. So he scraped off the mud, wiped them clean, and then put them to dry by the radiator.

At bedtime, Mother told him to tidy up, and he looked round the room at all the toys he had brought down to play with. There were drawing books and colouring pencils, six little cars, a bag of bricks, a teddy bear and a book about trains. And his shoes. David's arms were so full he could hardly see where he was going! First, the teddy bear fell off the top of the pile and he had to put down the bag of bricks to pick up the teddy. Then the brick-bag was so unsteady that it fell out of his arms. David put the shoes down to pick up the bricks, and the colouring pencils fell out of their case and went bouncing all over the floor. David began to get really cross.

'Why don't you put them all in a carrier-bag and take them all upstairs like that?' Mother called from the kitchen when she heard him grumbling.

'It's all right!' David shouted, and at last the things were all balanced in his arms again and he began to struggle up the stairs. Near the top he dropped one of his shoes. 'Oh bother!' he said, and went on into his bedroom. 'I'll pick that up in a minute!'

He dropped his great bundle into the toy-box. Teddy had fallen in head first, so he needed to be pulled out and propped up on the top, where he could watch David getting ready for bed. Two of the cars also spilled out of the cardboard box, and one of them rolled right under the bed. David crawled after it and threw it back into the box.

Now he must put on his pyjamas, wash his face and hands, and clean his teeth before Mother came up to read him a story. Back in the bedroom, David reached up for a favourite book from the book shelf, and was just climbing into bed when he heard Mother shut the kitchen door and begin to climb the stairs.

Suddenly there was a bump and a crash. David jumped out of bed.

'What's happened?' he called from the landing. Mother was sitting near the bottom of the stairs, rubbing her elbow. 'What are you doing there?' asked David.

Mother looked up at him. 'I fell over a shoe near the top,' she said. 'I didn't see it, and I fell. I bumped my arm rather badly on the wall as I went down. I think I've bruised it.'

A shoe! David remembered dropping that shoe. He had meant to go back and pick it up, but he had forgotten, and now Mother had tripped over it and had hurt herself. He felt sorry, very sorry. He should have thought what might happen. Perhaps he had not so much forgotten as not bothered to remember.

'I'll be more careful next time,' he promised, as he watched while Mother ran cold water over her bruised elbow. 'After all,' he thought to himself, 'Mother looks after me, so I really ought to look after her, as well.'

Giving presents

Project outline

Young children enjoy gifts, although they are often more concerned with receiving them than giving them! Talk about special times when the children look forward to presents: Christmas, birthdays and Easter, or perhaps when Father has been away on business, or when grandparents arrive to stay. Ask them to make pictures of, or write about, presents that they have been particularly pleased to receive. If there are any birthdays during the week, encourage the child(ren) concerned to bring their gifts and cards, and let them share their excitement and happiness with the whole group. Remind them that receiving and thanking go together.

Talk about the giving of presents. Ask if they can remember any that they have given to parents, brothers or sisters, grandparents, etc. Let them describe not only the gifts, but what the recipient said, or what their face looked like, at the time of giving. This will help the children to appreciate the pleasure that the gift gives to someone else. If they describe what are 'bought' gifts, such as talcum powder, bouquets of flowers, scarves, etc, ask *how* they were purchased. Did the child go with someone else to select the gift? Was it bought with the child's own money? At this point you might, as sensitively as possible, discover how some children save for presents, or perhaps pay for them with money earned by doing small jobs at home. How many of them are given money straight from their parents' purses to buy presents? How many of them have gifts chosen and bought for them by adults, so that all the child does is hand it over? This kind of giving, saving the parents an amount of time and talk, can lead to the child, when older, never expecting to pay in any way for things that are to be given to others.

Giving usually involves some kind of sacrifice. Try to analyse this for yourself: how many of us could more willingly spend the money, or time, upon ourselves?

Remind the children that not all giving requires money. We can also give time, and help, and care. Find out if the children do jobs around the house. Sometimes these are paid for, to supplement the pocket-money; if the children offered to do them for nothing, this would be a gift. Likewise, obeying an order to do something can become a kind of gift when done quickly and willingly. Let the

31

children suggest work that could be done by them at home, for nothing but love. The story given for use in the Assembly suggests ways of making time and help into real gifts. Consider the possibility of your children preparing similar 'gift sheets'.

Let the children make 'un-birthday' gifts or cards to take home. This shows that no one has to wait for special occasions for giving. Surprises are often received with more enjoyment.

Finally, think with your class about the very simple gift of pleasure itself, and ways in which this can be given. Smiles, politeness, obedience and unselfishness are all ways in which even the poorest of us can give—to those we love, to friends, and acquaintances, and even to strangers.

The Assembly

Hymns and songs

Father God, our gifts we bring	NCS 81
Here we come with gladness	NCS 82
He gave me eyes so I could see	SSL 19
Jesus' hands were kind hands	SSL 33

Poem

A present for Grandma

Grandma is old, but she still has a birthday;
Mum asked me what I'd like to give.
I thought of a banquet, or baskets of flowers,
or a new house in which she could live.
'But you haven't the money!' my Mum said to me.
'You couldn't afford to give that!'
So I thought of a book, or even some soap,
or a ribbon for Grandma's new hat.

I counted my pennies and went to the shop
at the end of our very long street;
but all they had got was packets of tea,
tins of dog food, and slices of meat.
No books and no ribbons, and only the soap
you use when you're scrubbing the floor;
'No, thank you, I'll leave it,' I said to the man,
and went home to think a bit more.

32

I thought I might knit her a warm, woolly hat,
but we hadn't got needles or wool,
and when I had knitted a scarf for my doll
it hadn't turned out very well.
'Go round to your Grandma's, and give her a treat,'
suggested my Mum on the day.
'Just give her a smile, and a kiss and a hug,
and wish her a happy birthday.'

I went; and I gave her a little bit more
'cos I laid her small table for tea;
and she let me make cakes for her specially to eat,
which she shared with her budgie and me.
So Grandma was happy, her day a success,
and all I had given her then
was some of my time, and lots of my love;
but I'm sure I shall do it again!

Prayer

Dear Lord God, we feel so pleased when we are given presents;
   help us to remember to say 'Thank you'.
We also like seeing people's faces when we give things to them.
   May we give our time, our love, and our happiness to others as well.
Thank you, dear God, for all the things you have given us in this wonderful
   world.
Thank you, thank you, for loving us so much.

Stories

Bible stories: Giving help, the good Samaritan—Luke 10.30-35
                     The widow's gift—Mark 12.41-44
Hannah's present (told in full)

Hannah's present

It was all quiet, and still dark, in Hannah's home. She knew she was the only one
awake, and she stretched her arms on the pillow and began to think her early-
morning thoughts.

Christmas was only two days away. Hannah's excitement trembled inside her
as she wondered what Mum and Dad had got for her present this year. She wanted
a doll's pram, or a bicycle, or a pair of roller skates, but she was afraid she would
not get any of these things. Dad was out of work, and they could only afford

33

things like food, and the rent for the flat, and second-hand clothes from jumble sales.

She thought about the presents she had ready to give to them, already wrapped up under her bed. At school she'd made a pincushion for mother, and there was a pot for putting pencils in for Dad. She had made that at home, following the instructions given on a children's TV programme. She had made a Christmas card as well, for her teacher, and now she only had to get a present for Grandma and Grandpa. But she had no money at all. Dad had stopped giving her pocket-money when he left work, and she knew Mum was saving every penny she could to buy Dad a thick, woolly scarf for Christmas. She just did not know what to do about Grandma and Grandpa, who had asked Mum and Dad and Hannah to their house for Christmas dinner. Hannah wanted to take something for them, but could not think what.

Then an idea started buzzing round in her head. It began when she remembered something her teacher had said at school. 'We can all give presents, and they don't have to cost a lot of money.' Hannah had not got even a little money, so she tried to remember what Miss Graham had said next. It was something about being able to give things like time and happiness. Well, Hannah had got time: two days before Christmas, and all the school holiday afterwards. She was happy, too, specially as it was near Christmas, so she might be able to give some of that away.

Hannah pushed back the sheets and jumped out of bed. She had no time to get dressed, or she would forget the good idea that was racing round in her head. She pulled on a cardigan, and a pair of thick socks, and crept downstairs. Mum had a note-pad in the kitchen, for writing shopping lists, and Hannah was sure she would not mind her taking a few sheets to make her present for Grandma and Grandpa. She found a pencil, then went up to her bedroom again, and shut the door. This was *her* secret; she did not want Mum and Dad even to guess what she was going to give her grandparents on Christmas Day.

Hannah got back into bed, because it was warmer to work there, and, with a book to rest on, she began to write on the first bit of paper. She added a little drawing, because the page seemed a bit empty, and then began on the second piece. When she had finished writing and drawing on five bits of paper she took the last piece and wrote the words 'Happy Christmas' in big letters on it, with 'love from Hannah' underneath them. The bits of paper were all the same size and shape, so she found a paper-clip and put them all together like a little book. There was a small piece of wrapping paper under her bed, which she put round the present, then tied it up with string.

'I've got a present for Grandma and Grandpa,' she told Mum and Dad at breakfast, 'but I'm not telling you what it is.'

Mother and Father wanted to guess, but Hannah kept her mouth tightly shut.

Christmas Day came at last, and Mum and Dad and Hannah went to church. Hannah loved the Christmas carols, and sang all the ones she had learnt at school. After it was over, they walked to Grandma and Grandpa's house.

Nobody could wait until after lunch for the presents to be given out, and besides, the Christmas dinner was taking a long time to cook. So they all sat round the gas fire and gave each other their gifts. Hannah thought that the present Mum and Dad gave her was rather strange: it was a little collar, only big enough for her teddy bear! She thought he would look very smart in it, mind you, but did teddy bears really wear collars?

Grandma and Grandpa took an awfully long time to open Hannah's present. They did not just rip off the string and tear away the paper, but undid the knot very carefully, then unwrapped the paper and folded it smoothly. At last they lifted up the six little pieces of paper all clipped together. Mother and Father moved closer so that they could see what the surprise present was. Grandma and Grandpa read the cover message then folded it back to read what was written on the next page. Hannah had written, *'I promise to visit you every Thursday after school.'*

'How lovely,' said Grandma. 'What a lovely present, Hannah.'

'It isn't finished yet,' said Hannah quickly.

Grandpa turned to the second sheet of paper. *'I promise to pick you the first daffodils from my garden,'* he read.

'Oh, Hannah,' said Grandma, and gave her a hug.

'Turn over to the next one,' said Hannah.

'I promise to sweep your garden path,' Grandpa read on the third page.

'Go on,' said Hannah, 'there's still some more!'

So Grandpa turned over another page and read, *'I promise to sing you a song this afternoon.'*

'Oh, good,' said Grandma, 'we'd love that!'

Grandpa had got to the last page. He read it aloud. *'I promise to love you always,'* it said.

Grandma held Hannah close and kissed her. Grandpa wiped his eyes and adjusted his specs. 'Must have caught a cold,' he said, and blew his nose.

'That was the very nicest Christmas present we have ever had,' said Grandma, and everybody cuddled each other in happiness.

'But we haven't given you your present, yet, Hannah,' Grandpa said. 'There's a big box in the hall. Go and see what you can find inside it.'

Hannah had seen the big box when she walked through the front door. She rushed out to look inside it. At first she thought it was only full of torn-up newspaper, but she knew there must be more than that! At last her fingers felt the present—something soft like a silken, fluffy ball, warm, and small, and—

breathing! Gently she lifted out a ball of silky white fluff, which had two blue eyes and the dearest little pink nose—a kitten! Hannah did not know how to say thank you—her heart felt too big, and her eyes were almost crying with joy! But she was smiling, and through the smile she whispered, 'Thank you! Thank you so very, very much!'

The kitten purred softly. 'I think I'll call him Mr Softy,' she said. She knew now what the tiny collar was for; not for her teddy bear, but for Mr Softy. Mum and Dad and Grandma and Grandpa must have been planning this special present together. She looked round the room at all the happy faces. How lovely it was to be able to give to each other!

The cold

Project outline

Take the opportunity of some really wintry weather to start work on this topic. It need not be snowing or very icy, although these products of a cold spell will be mentioned and can be enlarged upon as the project goes on. Choose one or more of the subjects suggested below as your main theme, but first spend a little time in general conversation about the cold. This should include: at what time of year we usually feel cold; what parts of our bodies feel the cold quickly; what we can do to warm up (eg, put on extra clothing, have warm food and drink, exercise, allow heat from fires or radiators to warm our bodies, and so on); what natural phenomena would tell us it was cold, even if we felt warm ourselves (ice, snow, breath vapour, etc). At this stage, do not elaborate in any one direction. Begin planning together how you will build an Assembly on the subject. What you go on to study will depend on the time at your disposal, the weather itself, and the particular interests and abilities of your children.

Frost and Ice   What is frost? If there has been a hoar frost overnight, take the children outside; does it feel very cold? Is there a wind blowing? What sort of clothes, including shoes, do we need to wear? Scrape a little of the white frost onto a dish and take it indoors; what happens to it? Owing to central heating, not many windows these days get the 'Jack Frost' patterns that older people knew in childhood, but there may be an outhouse, outside toilets, or shed, where they can be seen early in the morning. If so, let the children look at them with a magnifying glass to find out what the patterns are made of. Later you could decorate a classroom window in a similar way, using 'scrunched-up' cling film, or tissue-paper. When the boys and girls have realised that these patterns are made of ice, they may be able to suggest what happens to them when the room, shed, etc warms up.

If the children are old enough, explain how the patterns were formed; and take daily temperature readings, both indoors and out, and plot them. In icy conditions, the playground may have puddles which are iced over. Let the children touch the ice, find out how thick it is, notice reflections in it, and slide on it (if this is allowed) under supervision. Look for icicles, frozen pipes, and frozen washing left on lines; also at frost and ice on leaves, shrubs and trees. Look at breath vapour, during ordinary conversation, and when the children deliberately blow and pant.

If you are pursuing this subject, go on to find out about icebergs; animals that enjoy icy conditions; the uses for ice; ice skating, etc. Find out what happens to jars of tap-water—one of which also contains a large quantity of salt—left out overnight in icy weather. Talk about sand and salt being laid on the roads; and why the sea rarely freezes.

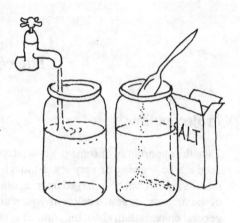

Snow If it is actually snowing, take the class out to feel the snow falling; what happens to it when it comes in contact with warm human bodies? Try to catch a snowflake on a dark, woolly cloth, and look at it with a magnifying glass, or through a microscope. Try to draw it, and count the number of sides each crystal has. If this is not possible, show pictures of magnified snowflakes; let the children draw them, and make patterns of them with folded and cut paper. If there is snow on the ground, let the children squeeze some together in their hands to form snowballs. What happens to the crystals? What happens if you take a snowball into a warm room? How long does it take to melt? Measure the depth of the snow, on two consecutive mornings if possible. Find out how snow is cleared for traffic. If you continue with this topic, find out about snow on mountain peaks; avalanches and glaciers; skiing and other winter sports; talk about hail and how it is formed.

God's care needs our help Discuss again how *we* feel the cold, and how we can get warm by running, waving our arms, clapping our hands, etc. Talk about old people, with bodies that are slowing down. How do they keep warm? What would happen if they fell on icy pavements that had been made more slippery by children sliding on them? Remind the class that extra, and hot, food makes us feel warmer. How do old people manage in this way? Talk about the people who help them, and the services they provide. Think together about outdoor workers—milkmen, postmen, builders, window cleaners, gardeners and farmers. How are their jobs affected by weather conditions? Consider some animal life and how it copes; perhaps you can feed some wild birds on a regular basis; ask at a local zoo or boarding kennels whether anything special has to be done there during very cold weather. Find out from farmers how frosty, snowy weather affects their work and their animals. Bring out how people show they care, both for other human beings, and for animals and birds.

During this study make sure you keep records, pictures and written work so that they may be used in some way during the Assembly.

The Assembly

Hymns and songs

In the winter birds need food	NCS 26
We thank you, loving Father God	NCS 27
See how the snowflakes are falling	NCS 28, SSL 57
To God who makes all lovely things	
(verses 1, 3, 5)	SSL 9

Poem (This could be spoken with actions)

Cold Weather

Icy wind
sometimes blows;
when it does—
cold nose;
and when skies
bring the snows,
you can get
cold toes!

Rub your hands,
stamp your feet,
have some toast
to eat;
run about
and you'll beat
snow and ice,
and sleet.

Some who're old
and house-bound,
can't move fast
around;
think of them
when you've found
snow is on
the ground.

Just a smile
makes them glow,
when cold winds
do blow;
think of ways,
let them know,
then your care
will show.

Music

Waltz of the Snowflakes from *Nutcracker Suite*, Tchaikovsky
Sleigh Ride, LeRoy Anderson
(For use as background and atmosphere music)

39

Dear Father God,
in icy weather
we bow our heads
in prayer together.

Keep safe, we pray,
in cold and snow,
all those who work
when cold winds blow.
May people care
a little more
for those who're ill,
or old, or poor.

And give us time
in all our fun
to bring a bit
of warming sun
to those who live
in loneliness.
All who need help,
dear Father, bless.

Stories

Bible stories: Verses from a psalm—Psalm 147.1, 15-18
Paul camps in the cold—Acts 28.1-2
The first snow (told in full)

The first snow

It was Sadhana's first winter in England. In the summer she had come all the way from Pakistan with her parents to live in a big town not many miles from London. Sadhana's Uncle Aran had bought a grocer's shop in the town, and he had asked Mother and Father to come over and help him work in it. Sadhana had come from a country where it was always hot, even in winter-time, and when the family arrived in August, Sadhana found that England was hot, too, and she was pleased. But as the weeks went by, she began to feel the cold. Father bought her a thick cardigan and warm, woolly tights; Mother made her hot curries to eat, and Uncle Aran fixed an electric heater in their little first floor flat.

When Sadhana woke one morning in winter, it seemed to be extra light. She pulled back the curtains and could hardly believe her eyes! The whole world had changed, as if by magic! The roof-tops over the town were white, the tree in the garden below was bent and hanging with white, and the ground had a cotton wool carpet.

Mother was boiling milk on the gas stove.

'Have you seen the new town?' asked Sadhana. 'I want to go out in it!'

'It's very cold,' said Mother. 'I thought it would snow last night.'

So this was snow, Sadhana thought. She had seen snow on the top of the mountains in the far distance at home in Pakistan; it looked beautiful, but very far away. Now, snow was very near. Sadhana rushed to open the front door.

'What *are* you doing?' asked Father, coming into the room. 'We shall perish with cold if you open the door!'

'But I want to be in the snow! I want to feel it, to taste it, to listen to it!' Sadhana said.

'Silly child,' said Father. 'How can you hear the snow? And you're certainly not going out in it without something warm inside you—and warmer clothes on your outside, too!'

Sadhana drank her hot milk, then put on her coat and the thick boots they had bought only last Saturday in the market. Mother took her long silk scarf and tied it round Sadhana's head and neck. 'Stay in the garden,' she called as Sadhana slipped out into the cold, and down the steps into the garden.

Sadhana stood and looked at the snow. The sun was shining, and all the shadows in the garden were blue. The snow was sparkly white; somehow it smoothed out the garden, like a blanket smoothed out the shape of her body in bed, thought Sadhana. She walked into the snow; her toes felt cold, even inside her new warm boots. She picked up a handful of the lovely white crystals. They lay, cold and glittering, in her hand, then, before her very eyes, melted into water. Sadhana stumped on through the snow to the tree. One branch was so low that she almost bumped into it. She put her mouth forward and took a bite at the snow. It was like ice cream, only not sweet and creamy like the ones they sold in the shop. And it was gone so quickly. She stood still and listened; she could hear cars going by at the front of the shops, but they were much quieter than usual, as if their tyres wore woolly socks. Everything else was quiet and very, very still.

A robin hopped from one branch to another in the tree, so lightly that the snow did not move. He looked at Sadhana with his head on one side. Sadhana had seen him before, and had watched while he drank from the puddles on the garden path, or poked his beak into Father's newly-dug vegetable garden. Today the puddles and vegetable garden could not be seen; did the robin think he had come to some magical land too?

'Isn't it lovely?' Sadhana asked the robin. The robin's black eye looked back at her, and he ruffled himself until he looked like a brown feathery ball. She wondered what he would eat on a day when the world had turned white. Perhaps he needed help.

Sadhana went back up the steps to the flat, and the robin watched her, hopping to another branch to see her better.

'I need food to keep me warm,' Sadhana said to her mother, 'so can I take out a bit of bread to keep the robin warm?'

Mother gave her a saucer, and a slice of bread to break into crumbs. 'You'd better take a little bowl of water for him, too,' she said.

Sadhana carried the robin's breakfast out very quietly so that she would not frighten him away. She balanced the bowl and the saucer on the little table where she had eaten her tea back in the warm summer days. Today she had to sweep the snow off the top with her fingers. Oh, it was cold! The robin stayed where he was, watching.

'Sadhana!' called Father from the window. 'It's time to have your breakfast and get off to school.'

Sadhana wished the robin would hop down to his breakfast first, but she had to turn and go back into the building, climbing the stone steps to the flat.

'The robin didn't want the food,' she said sadly.

'I think he did,' said Father. 'Look now.'

Sadhana looked out of the window. The robin was standing on the saucer with crumbs of bread all round him. He looked up at the window.

'I think he's saying thank you,' said Mother.

Sadhana smiled. She was sure his beak opened in a smile—and she was almost sure he winked at her!

Christmas peace

Project outline

Traditionally, and theoretically, Christmas is a time of peace and goodwill. Towards the end of the autumn term these ideals may be far from reality as the school bustles busily nearer its Christmas parties, plays and concerts with mounting excitement. The atmosphere can transform even the most timid child into a human firework, so that by the end of term the display of rockets, squibs and catherine wheels seems unending! We look for peace, we long for peace, and we are apprehensive that peace will never return.

Once the term ends, many teachers prepare frenziedly for their own family Christmas, shopping for food and presents in the tangle of human life that has tipped into town and city alike. We may cry, like Paula in the story, 'Where is peace?' To embark on a project on the subject of peace at this time may seem to some to be insanity. To others it may hold out the hope of restraint and of moments of calm so needed in the school day as Christmas approaches. To make it work at all we need to be quite clear what we aim to show the children: that there are different kinds of peace, which all have common factors and which can all lead to the same understanding of the word.

Peace after war With the constant troubles in Northern Ireland, Central America and the Middle East, the children must be aware of fighting in other parts of the world. Television brings the horror of war into their living-rooms, and not many children aged 5-8 can be so sheltered that they cannot produce graphic illustrations of war if asked. Talk about these conflicts with the children; you may find that some are filled with excitement as they imagine the fighting and the winning of the battles. Point out that the fighting armies are under the orders of the rulers of their nations. Peace, therefore, depends not on the cessation of fighting between particular groups of soldiers but on positive moves of governments and rulers. Peace talks that lead to peace treaties lead to a cessation of hostilities at the battlefront, and then the nations concerned are at peace.

Peace between people On a level nearer the children's understanding we can find many examples of this type of peace, especially after playground fights or quarrels. Children can become involved in quite bitter and complex arguments which can lead to many forms of physical violence and torment. When stopped and separated by adults, peace reigns once more; an uneasy peace perhaps, and one that may not last because the beginnings of it are never sorted out by 'peace talks'.

Fighting children, either individuals or groups, disrupting the rough-and-tumble of the playground will, of course, be stopped. But once in the class-room again, bring the whole class together for a frank discussion. Point out that once there had been an intervention between the battling playground parties, then there was, on the surface, peace. To maintain that peace, peace talks should begin. Listen to the grievances without taking sides, and lead those concerned to think of ways in which the differences could be settled and further fighting avoided. Ask the rest of the class for their suggestions; some children may come up with solutions not thought of previously.

Peace around us Without trying to draw any parallels in the states of 'peace' at this stage, find a moment (and there will be many!) when the noise level in the class-room has risen to unacceptable heights. Then ask for peace. 'Quiet! Give me some peace!' may be all that is needed. When there is silence, talk about it and discuss this type of peace, which is not a cessation of hostilities, between nations or individuals, but a period of quiet. Ask the children to listen for sounds they would have missed in the previous hubbub. At this point, older children could be encouraged to write a poem about peace—any kind of peace. Younger ones could draw or paint pictures of times when they felt peaceful—full of peace.

Peace on the earth Now go on to the Christmas story, concentrating on the experience of the shepherds when they heard the song of the angels. Read it to the children, and see if they pick up the relevant words about peace: 'Glory to God in highest heaven, and on earth his peace.' (Luke 2.14, NEB) God's peace, as St Paul wrote, is 'beyond our utmost understanding'. (Philippians 4.7, NEB) God's peace must surely be there when wars have ceased, physical fighting has ended in friendship, and man's inmost mental and spiritual conflicts have been placed in God's keeping. Many aspects of peace have their beginnings at Christmas when most people have goodwill and glad anticipation in their hearts. Perhaps that is what this project should aim at—the beginning of a peace that will bring lasting results as the boys and girls grow older.

Peace is a positive quality. It is not merely a cessation of hostilities. It is a building and making and doing; it is stepping forward instead of standing still; it is an offering.

The Assembly

Hymns and songs

Away in a manger	NCS 48
Softly sleeping, softly sleeping	NCS 49
Little Jesus, sweetly sleep	NCS 50
While shepherds watched their flocks by night	

Poem

Christmas Peace

Here, Jesus, we stand still,
we want our hearts to fill
  with peace today:
peace that you promised then,
peace between fighting men,
peace in the world again,
  dear Lord, we pray.

Peace you have come to bring,
let all the church bells ring
  when Christmas starts.
And when the day is done,
when all the songs are sung,
after the noise and fun,
  peace in our hearts.

Music

Fantasia on Christmas Carols, Vaughan Williams
Pastoral Symphony from *Christmas Oratorio,* J. S. Bach
(Two less-used pieces of Christmas music evoking peace)

Prayer

Think about the stable where Jesus was born, and how quiet it was after the busy streets of Bethlehem. Think of the rustle of the straw while Joseph made a soft bed for Mary. Think of their quiet whispers, and of the little cry the baby made after he was born.

Lord Jesus, in all the excitement of our Christmas we are being very quiet and still so that we can think about you. Thank you for this peace. When we are in the middle of a lot of noise, help us to remember your peace, and to carry it in our hearts.

Stories

Bible story: On earth his peace—Luke 2.8-16
Give me peace! (told in full)

Give me peace!

All the others were in the big playroom. Simon and Jenny were arguing about where to put a silver star on the Christmas tree, Peter and Big Richard were hanging the last of the paper chains, with Katy holding the bottom of Peter's ladder, and Little Richard was standing in the middle of the floor, screaming. Paula did not like it when Little Richard screamed, so she dropped her long tinsel streamer and ran into the lounge.

The television was on in there, so Paula sat down to watch it. She was glad to be quiet and alone for once. In the family Children's Home it was difficult to find space to be by yourself. There was always noise and bustle, and talk and arguments. But there were also many times when there was fun and laughter, when they all watched a good television programme together, or Auntie Marge got them together by the fire to read them a story.

Paula had been in the Children's Home for three years, ever since she was four years old. Only Big Richard had been there longer, and he was twelve now. Auntie Marge and Uncle John looked after them like a Mum and Dad; it was just like living in a very big family.

The news-reader on the television was talking about a war that was being fought somewhere on the other side of the world. There were pictures of soldiers and aeroplanes and guns, and a reporter was talking about the fighting, and about some peace talks that had broken down. Paula did not want to listen, so she got up and went to find Auntie Marge in the kitchen. Auntie Marge was making mince pies for the Christmas dinner.

'Have you come to help me, Paula?' she asked, and Paula thought that would be fun.

'Can I make the pastry circles?' she said, picking up the round pastry cutter with the curly edge. Auntie Marge had the radio on, and music filled the big kitchen. It was warm in the kitchen, and when Paula heard the carols being sung she felt warm inside as well.

'All glory be to God on high,
       And to the earth be peace ...' the choir sang.

'What is peace?' Paula asked Auntie Marge. The man on the television had said that peace talks had broken down.

'It's when people can live in a friendly way, and not fight each other,' said Auntie Marge, who knew all about the war.

Just at that minute they heard Uncle John's key in the front door. The children had been waiting for him to come home. Katy and Jenny rushed for a cuddle, Peter and Big Richard grabbed his hands to drag him towards the playroom, Simon shouted about the Christmas tree, and Little Richard screamed again. Paula pushed her way towards Uncle John, calling, 'I'm making mince pies with Auntie Marge. Come and look!'

'Here, wait a minute,' gasped Uncle John. 'Give me a break! I want a bit of peace for a moment. Where's Auntie Marge?'

Paula stopped shouting. A bit of peace! Where was this peace? She thought it was over on the other side of the world, waiting to begin. She thought of the carol, 'And to the earth be peace . . .'. Perhaps it was everywhere, waiting to be noticed, like the rain outside the window.

'Where is peace?' she asked Uncle John.

'Certainly not here at the moment!' said Uncle John, going into the playroom to sort out a quarrel between Simon and Big Richard. 'That's enough, you two,' he ordered, and the room was suddenly quiet.

'Is that peace?' asked Paula, standing in the middle of the silence.

Uncle John took her through to the lounge. He switched off the television. 'Yes,' he said, 'that's one kind of peace. No noise; like when we go up to the big meadow together and sit in the long grass. No one about, and only being able to hear the grasshoppers and the wind blowing. That's peace.'

'No fighting is peace, too,' said Paula.

'Yes, when a country finishes fighting with another there is peace,' agreed Uncle John. 'But peace isn't always no noise, or no fighting. In those two things people have *stopped* doing something, and it can seem quite empty. Sometimes, peace means *doing* things. Perhaps you'll see what I mean on Christmas Day.'

Christmas came at last, and everyone was excited. They ripped open presents with squeals of delight, and everyone shouted 'Thank you!' and 'Just what I wanted!' to each other. Paula waited for the Christmas Day peace to arrive. It didn't come when they sang carols at the top of their voices at ten o'clock, nor when they played rushing-round games at eleven. Everyone was happy, though, and even Little Richard wasn't screaming. Paula held his hand when they went in for Christmas dinner. 'Would you sit next to me?' she asked him, and he gave her a huge smile. Simon stood by Uncle John, rushing the plates he was filling with roast turkey to Auntie Marge who piled on vegetables and stuffing. Big Richard showed Katy how to blow up the balloon from her Christmas cracker, and Peter was reading Jenny's motto to her. When Little Richard spilt his orange juice on the table, no one teased him about it, and Paula went for a cloth. It was a noisy dinner, everyone talking to each other, and laughing at jokes they would not have found at all funny the day before.

After dinner, Uncle John suggested a walk on the Downs for a breath of fresh sea air. They needed thick coats and stout shoes, as it was cold. Katy held Little Richard's wellington boots so that he could step into them fast, and Paula did up his buttons.

It was a lovely walk. They had a competition to see whose white breath lasted longest in the winter air when they breathed out; Uncle John raced Big Richard and Peter all the way from the farm gate to the cliff steps. When Uncle John won, Peter did not say, as he usually did, 'It's not fair!' but went up to Uncle John and said, 'Great stuff!'

After a Christmas-cake tea, when it was getting dark, Auntie Marge suggested some more carols. Uncle John played the piano for them and everyone sang softly. Paula was sleepily happy. Auntie Marge found her Bible and began to read the Christmas story, and Paula crept near to see the pictures. Auntie Marge was reading about the angels who gave the shepherds a big surprise by telling them baby Jesus had been born. 'They all sang praises together,' read Auntie Marge. ' "Glory to God in highest heaven, and on earth his peace." '

Paula was wide awake again. Peace! She'd forgotten that it might be there on Christmas Day! Perhaps she'd missed it! 'Have we had peace today?' she asked Uncle John.

'Yes, Paula, it was here all right,' he said. 'It was here when you were all playing well together, and being kind to each other, and laughing at each other's jokes. It was here when you were helping each other, and when you spoke to each other politely. *That* was peace—a *doing* peace!'

Paula thought she understood. She had enjoyed that kind of peace. She wished the people who fought wars knew about it. She looked round the room. Simon and Katy and Jenny sat on the settee watching Little Richard trying to balance on his big red ball; they were smiling and helping him not to fall. Big Richard was looking at Peter's new telescope and giving him hints on how to use it. Uncle John had gone to help Auntie Marge get the evening cocoa ready. Peace was everywhere, and everyone was *doing* it. It felt very good.

48

A child of Palestine

Project outline

This project gives scope for providing the children with some knowledge of Bible times. The story leads naturally out of the research into how people lived in New Testament times. Notes are given about houses, animals, food and clothing at the time of Jesus. These give basic material to begin the project, which might culminate in a model Palestinian village, a frieze of village life, or a scrap-book of drawings and writing about the subject, all of which could be displayed at the Assembly.

Houses Because of the heat, houses in Palestine were built of thick stone; the windows were usually small, and had no glass. Most houses were square or rectangular, with outside stairs leading up to a flat roof, which was surrounded by a parapet for safety. The roof was in constant use as an extra room: fruit was laid out to dry in the sun, home-made cheese was left to thicken and harden, and clothes were spread out to dry. It was also a meeting-place for friends and relatives after the day's work was done. Inside the houses of poor people the hard dried-mud floor had a raised platform at one end where the family slept and had their meals. Wealthy merchants, government officials and land-owners had houses that were bigger and more elaborate, often built round a courtyard garden.

Animals Cattle, sheep and goats were important and valuable to the farmer, as his livelihood largely depended on the milk, skin, wool and flesh that animals provided. Cattle were used for the heavy work of ploughing the fields and threshing the corn. Poor men might keep only one or two sheep or goats; richer farmers might own several pairs of oxen or flocks of sheep, and employ farm workers and shepherds to look after them. Almost every family, even the poorest, owned a donkey, as these animals ate far less than horses, and could carry extremely heavy loads.

Food Bread, the staple food, was made from barley or wheat flour and baked in tall clay ovens, or sometimes over an open fire. Leaven, or yeast, was used to make the bread rise, but for unexpected guests, or a hurried meal, unleavened bread was baked.

Milk, from the cattle or goats, was hard to keep fresh in the hot climate and was only used for the young children. Most was made into a kind of yoghurt, or an oily butter, or thickened for cheese. Sometimes diluted camel's milk was drunk.

Near sea-shore or lake, fish, eaten fresh, or salted down to preserve it, became a large part of the people's diet. The Sea of Galilee provided most of the fish available.

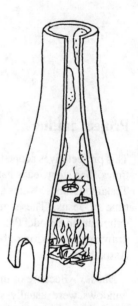

Vegetables such as lentils, cucumbers, marrows and melons, were grown for food and eaten mainly in thick stews called pottage. The main fruits were figs, dates and grapes, but pomegranates were also plentiful. Wine was made from the grapes, which were also eaten raw, or dried to form raisins and used extensively as sweetening. Oil was necessary in cooking, and this was produced by crushing the olives which grew, and still grow, in profusion in the olive groves.

Clothes Loose, flowing garments are the most suitable for the hot climate of the Middle East. Poor people wore shapeless tunics, the men's either full-length or short, and belted with leather. The women wore long robes with a sash at the waist. Over this, a thick woollen cloak or coat was worn, which doubled as a night-time blanket, and was precious enough to warrant laws as to its ownership and use. Heads were usually covered with squares of cloth as protection against the blazing sun. Open leather sandals were worn on the feet.

These notes give only the barest details of some aspects of life in New Testament times. There is a wealth of information in other books which interested teachers should study before embarking on this project. (See the *Getting to Know About* Series, NCEC)

The Assembly

Hymns and songs

When Jesus was a little boy	NCS 57
I love to think that Jesus saw	NCS 59
Happy laughter, jolly games	NCS 61
Now Jesus one day	SSL 30

Poem (Use models or pictures with the poem, if possible)

The loaf of bread

Here is the bread that Jesus gave
to hungry people, when
they'd listened to his stories till
the sun went down again.
The corn that grew around, so gold,
was cut, and threshed, and ground
into the flour that women mixed,
with water, to a mound.
The dough was kneaded, just like this,
then flattened from a ball
to make a kind of pancake
put in an oven tall.
Watch the smoke come out the top,
the bread is baked right through,
then, if you add some raisins,
the bread is sweeter, too.

A little boy had bread like this,
and fish—a picnic meal—
when Jesus began asking
for food up on that hill.
The little boy gave willingly,
and Jesus, he was glad
to see the people sharing
the picnic that boy had.

Music

By the Rivers of Babylon (Psalm 137), Boney M
Hebrew Melody, opus 35, Achron
(The first sings a well-known psalm to a modern tune; the second evokes the
form of Hebrew music associated with Palestine.)

Stories

Bible story: The boy's picnic—John 6.5,8-11
How Joel got better (told in full)

How Joel got better

There was once a little boy—we'll call him Joel—who lived in Palestine a long,
long time ago. He lived in a fairly big house, which had an indoor garden, and his

51

family kept servants to prepare all the meals and to wait at table. Joel went to school every day, and to the synagogue every week. He wore good clothes and had good toys.

One day Joel felt far from well. His head ached, and although it was so hot outside, he shivered with cold. He wrapped his warm woollen coat tightly round him, and walked out to look for his father.

'It's cold,' he grumbled to his father who was sheltering from the sun in the courtyard.

'Nonsense!' said his father. 'It's hotter than ever today.'

'Well, I'm cold,' said Joel, and his teeth began to chatter, to prove it.

His father took a good look at him, and put a hand on his forehead. 'You look hot to me,' he said. 'Come on, lad, get on your bed. I'll send a servant in to give you water and make you comfortable.'

Joel was glad to lie down. His eyes hurt, and he was longing to close them and sleep. If only he did not feel so cold! He slept a little, then woke up hot and sweating. His mother was bending over him.

'Lie still, little Joel,' she said. 'You're rather ill, I'm afraid.' She soaked a cloth and laid it on his closed eyes. Joel slept again, then woke suddenly, still feeling as if he were in the middle of a really nasty dream.

Two days later his mother and father were getting very worried. Joel was no better; in fact, he seemed to be getting worse. He did not want to talk, he could not eat, and he tossed and turned on his bed, not even bothering to look up when his parents spoke to him.

Father took Mother to one side of the little room and whispered to her. 'Jesus, the healer, is in Cana,' he told her. 'The corn merchant told me so this morning. Said he can make people better. I'm going over there to ask him to come back with me to look at Joel.'

'It's about twenty miles*!' said Joel's mother in alarm. 'It'll take at least a day and a half to get there! Then, if you can find Jesus at all, you've got to persuade him to journey back with you all that way!'

'I *must* go!' said Joel's father. 'Joel will probably die within a week if we don't get help!'

In half an hour's time he had set off on the long road over the hills from Capernaum to Cana. When at last Cana was in sight, Joel's father was terribly tired, but he could not rest until he had found Jesus, the man who made people better.

'Have you seen Jesus?' he asked again and again. And then someone pointed to the hills above the village.

'He's up there,' he said.

Joel's father bowed low when at last he found himself standing before Jesus.

'It's my little boy,' he said, gasping for breath. 'He's very, very ill. Just lies there and moans. He'll die unless you can get to Capernaum with me quickly.'

Jesus looked at him. Joel's father was a rich man. Did he just want to boast to his rich friends that he had managed to drag the healer all the way to Capernaum to heal his sick son? But Joel's father was so worried that his words rushed out. 'Come with me, please come with me! I love my son, and I don't want him to die!'

Jesus was still standing there, calm and quiet. 'You go home,' he said at last. 'Your little boy is going to get well.'

Joel's father felt at once that what Jesus said was true. Joel *would* get better. 'Thank you, thank you,' was all he could say as he turned to go down the hill and journey back to Capernaum.

As soon as the big lake near his home was in sight, Joel's father was met by his own servants, hurrying over the fields towards him.

'It's all right, sir!' they shouted. 'He's getting better! He's not going to die.'

The father stood still on the stubbly grass. He was trembling with happiness and with thanks. 'When did he start to better?' he asked.

'About lunch-time yesterday,' said one of the servants. 'Just sat up and asked for a drink of water,' said the other. 'He was weak still, but he wasn't burning up with a fever any more.'

About lunch-time! Joel's father found it difficult to believe, but it was just about lunch-time yesterday when he had climbed the hill in Cana to find Jesus. Just about lunch-time when Jesus had said, 'Your little boy is going to get well.' Joel's father knelt down on the grass. 'Thank you, Jesus,' was all he could say.

* or thirty kilometres

Prayer
> Dear Jesus, we have been thinking about the country where you were born and where you grew up. We have heard stories about the kind of people you knew, and loved, and helped. We love you, Lord Jesus, and want you for our friend.

Being tidy

Project outline

More often than not young children are careless about putting things away after using them, and many teachers find it difficult to keep a tidy class-room. Much depends upon home training: an untidy house will produce an untidy child, although it is interesting to note that often it is these children who become fastidious adults, presumably rebelling against the untidiness with which they grew up!

The work leading up to the Assembly should result in a tidy class-room, at least for a time, and hopefully for much longer. Probably the best theme for the week would be 'A place for everything'.

Look at the boxes and containers in your class-room: are they in need of repair? Do they actually encourage the children to use them, by their appearance, strength and suitability? Could some be replaced, existing ones brightened and relabelled, and extra ones put in place? The contents of those already in use could be turned out and put back tidily after the boxes have been brushed out and cleaned. Look, with the children, at the shelves round the room. Do they look neat? Are they labelled? Consider the cupboards: does everything tend to fall out when the doors are opened? Find ways of improving the look of the room, discussing these with the children. Does the hamster cage, or the goldfish bowl, need cleaning out more thoroughly than usual? Do low curtains need washing, or round-the-room table-tops and display units need scrubbing or covering?

Get the children to relabel areas of the room, eg, the library, wendy-house, sand tray, etc. Think of new words to put in new places. Ask some children to count and check the books. Rearranging the room in some way, deciding together whether to move furniture, or have new sites for books etc, might lead to greater tidiness or make for more efficiency of work or ease of access. Make a special point of, and leave more time than usual for, clearing up after any work is done.

At intervals during this clearing up period, remind the children of the importance of keeping other places tidy, eg, the school toilets and wash-rooms and playground. Talk about litter in the streets, and about the places where litter can be disposed of. Ask them to count the litter-bins they see on their next visit to the town centre, get them to notice the designs and shapes of the bins, and where they are situated. A friendly dustman or bin-man could be invited to talk about his work and about any ways in which this work could be made easier by the people who expect him to collect their rubbish. Find out if there are special tips in the locality for the disposal of garden waste, or for items such as old beds and mattresses, cookers, etc.

Older children could explore further what actually happens to glass bottles, plastic containers, etc, when they have been thrown into the dustbin; or find out how kitchen waste can be used on compost heaps. Country schools could enquire about what happens to animal and vegetable waste on farms. If you are near a factory or a hospital or large restaurant, someone might come to talk about what happens to the rubbish there.

At the end of this preparation time for the Assembly, remind the children of the Genesis story of the creation; of how, when God created each part of the world, we are told that 'he looked and saw that it was good'. God does not want us to spoil his world by our carelessness or thoughtlessness.

The Assembly

Hymns and songs

God, who made the earth	NCS 6
Milk bottle tops and paper bags	SSL 17
The flowers that grow in the garden	SSL 53

Poem

It's up to me

Yesterday at tea-time
   the jam dripped down the jar,
and Mummy grumbled, on and on,
   'How careless, child, you are!'

Last night I left my toys
   before I went to bed;
'This room's a tip, so come right back,
   and clear up, child,' Dad said.

Today I came to school
   eating a squashy sweet;
'Now put the paper in the bin,
   and leave a tidy street.'

I thought my Mum and Dad
would clear things up, you see;
but now I realise that
the clearer-upper's me!

I suppose it is right
that I should do my best
to clear up rubbish I have left,
not leave it to the rest.

And if we all did this
God's world would be a place
much nicer to be lived in
by all the human race.

Music

The Sorcerer's Apprentice, Dukas
(The story behind this exciting piece of music is what can happen when our actions do have an effect on someone else's work!)

Prayer

We love your world, dear Father God; we would not like to see it dirty and spoiled. Help us to keep our part of it tidy and clean, so that everyone can enjoy it.

Stories

Bible story: God saw that it was good—Genesis 1; read from *Winding Quest* by Alan Dale, if possible

It's only rubbish! (told in full)

It's only rubbish!

Mrs Shaddock was in a hurry to go out. She bustled about the kitchen, washing the tea dishes and clearing away the food.

'Winston!' she shouted. 'Come and dry the plates for me.'

'Oh, leave them, Mum,' said Winston from his chair in front of the television set.

'Now, Winston, you know I like to make sure the kitchen's neat and tidy before Mrs Green comes over to baby-sit,' Mrs Shaddock said. She would be late for work, and it would be the second time that week. There was always so much to do at home first.

The telephone rang. 'Answer that for me, please, Winston,' she called.

Winston lifted the receiver, listened, spoke a few words, then shouted to his mother, 'It's Mrs Green. Her husband's come home from work ill, and she can't leave him. She won't be coming to sit with me this evening.'

Mrs Shaddock sat down at the kitchen table. 'Oh, Winston,' she said, 'what am I to do now?'

'Not go to work, I suppose,' said Winston. 'Your job's only clearing up rubbish, anyway. Not much of a job!'

'But I've got to go,' said his mother. 'They're depending on me to do it. I'd better take you with me.'

Winston brightened. His mother worked at the airport, and he had only been there once before. Perhaps he would see some planes taking off or landing. He jumped up, scattering biscuit crumbs onto the floor, and knocking down a newspaper. He decided to wear his blue anorak, but it was underneath his school blazer; he tried to unhook it, but the blazer fell down first, and got trodden on.

'Where are my shoes?' he called.

'You took them up to your bedroom, Winston,' said his mother. 'Do hurry up or we shan't catch the bus!'

Winston left his slippers in the hall and rushed upstairs for his shoes. One was under the bed, and the other was on the bed.

At last they were on the bus on the way to the airport. Winston was really excited, but it was almost dark, and he knew he would not be able to see many planes; never mind, there were always interesting people to watch.

When they went into the big building Mother went to tell someone she had arrived and to collect her overall, dustpan and large sweeping brush.

'You sit there, Winston,' she said when she came back. She put a packet of crisps into his hand, and Winston pulled at it, scattering a few crumbs on the floor as it burst open.

He watched while Mother took her long broom and started to sweep. Lots of people were walking past and round her, some pushing trolleys full of luggage, others with families of children and grannies; some were rushing, some were looking for friends, some were just standing in the way, waiting.

Mother's broom went backwards and forwards, gathering in bits of paper, dust, bits of string, old paper cups and forgotten magazines. When her pile was all pulled together she transferred it to the big black rubbish bag she had been given, and then started all over again. Winston could not believe it: even in the very same spot where she had just swept there were more sweet wrappers, old cartons, and this time an empty fizzy-drink can! How careless people were, how dirty! Now and again Mother took something and popped it into the big litter bin nearby. He watched as she pushed down the rubbish inside the bin to make room

57

for more. A man rushed past and flung his paper cup at the bin, but he missed, and it went rolling about on the floor. Wearily, Winston's mother bent down to pick it up. Winston noticed a boy eating an apple. When he had finished, he bent down and threw the apple core under his seat. Mother had to ask him to move a little as she fished for it with her broom.

Winston began to get cross. How dare all these people make so much mess for his mother to clear up? He rolled his empty crisp packet into a ball and threw it at the boy who had dropped the apple core. It hit a passing lady, who stopped to give Winston a frown. Mother appeared at that moment and whoosh! her broom had swept away his empty crisp packet.

By nine o'clock Winston was almost asleep. He blinked at Mother, who was still sweeping up rubbish from the same spot. 'Just going to get my coat, Winston,' she said as she passed him. 'We must get home and pop you into bed.'

As they sat on the bus on the way home, Winston said, 'Those people were awful, leaving all that rubbish about for you to clear up! They could easily have put it in the litter bin, couldn't they?'

'I seem to remember having to sweep up your crisp crumbs, and the bag your crisps came in, Winston,' said Mother. 'It's not just other people, you know, it's you as well!'

Winston did not think that was fair. He had only left one piece of rubbish lying about; you could not count the crumbs. Then he thought of the boy's apple core. He had only thrown away *one* piece of rubbish, too. And that man with the paper cup, and the lady who had left a magazine lying on her seat. He began to work it out. If everyone—and that meant him as well—had put their one bit of rubbish in the bin, how much easier his mother's job would have been, and how much cleaner the whole airport would have looked!

As they went through their own front door, Winston fell over his slippers and then saw his blazer lying on the floor. In the sitting-room the newspaper was where he had let it slide, and the biscuit crumbs showed up on the dark carpet. Usually he would have let Mother pick up everything, but tonight he bent down himself and put everything away. Already his own house looked tidier and more pleasant, and his mother could go straight to her armchair and sit down. He now knew that it was an awfully tiring job picking up other people's rubbish!

Pancake Day

Project outline

Shrove Tuesday gets its name from the word *shriven* or *shrived*, which means forgiveness of one's sins. Many years ago people went to church on the day before Lent began, to be forgiven for their past sins. The day was also a day of feasting before the fasting imposed by Lent.

There are many customs connected with this day. Some should be talked about, and perhaps dramatised.

Most children will know about the eating of pancakes, although the custom will be new to many immigrants. But few children will have any idea about the origins of this tradition. As Lent was a time for self-denial, and fasting, rich foods were eaten up before it began, and pancakes were an ideal way of using up eggs and butter. If there are suitable facilities, let the children assemble pancake ingredients, beat them together, and watch them cook. Sugar and lemons would add the final touches to the tasting! The boys and girls will no doubt remind you that pancakes need to be tossed, which will cause entertainment and amusement!

Other customs connected with the day, which still survive in parts of the country, include the pancake race at Olney, in Buckinghamshire. Housewives, carrying a cooked pancake in a frying-pan, race from the Market Square to the Parish Church, a distance of 350 metres (400 yards), and the pancakes must be tossed *en route*. The winner receives a prayer book and a kiss from the vicar. The race is followed by a service in the church, with all the frying-pans propped against the altar. The medieval origin of this race is that when the church bell rang on Shrove Tuesday all pancakes were supposed to have been made. One lady was behind with her cooking, heard the church bell ringing, and hurried off to the service, only to realise on her arrival that she was still wearing her apron and carrying her frying-pan containing the almost-cooked pancake! The 'Pancake Bell' can still be heard in many parishes on Shrove Tuesday.

Some communities and schools in towns and villages still hold other traditional pancake customs; some of these involve tossing the pancake over a high bar (Westminster School), shaking uncooked eggs in a sieve until only one is left whole (Stoke-by-Gregory, Somerset), skipping in Scarborough, and the making of special Shrovetide 'coquille buns' in Norwich.

59

Try to find pictures of Mardi Gras celebrations in some of the Spanish or French-speaking countries, and talk about them. It might be possible to hire a film of the Mardi Gras (Fat Tuesday) carnival in New Orleans. Any 'pretzels' or 'semlors' that can be found in baker's shop or delicatessen will make interesting exhibits of Shrovetide food special to Italy and Sweden respectively.

(The Easter Book, published by NCEC, contains further information.)

The Assembly

Hymns and songs

I'd like to be a milkman	NCS 34
The golden cockerel	SSL 2
The flowers that grow in the garden	SSL 53

Poem

Pancakes

Sift the flour,
  see it fly,
like a snowstorm
  from the sky.

Break the eggs,
  make a well,
drop them slowly,
  milk as well.

Fold and mix,
  stir and beat;
put the frying pan
  on the heat.

Ladle in,
  wait a bit;
toss and turn, then
  sugar it.

Lemon juice
  sprinkled on;
taste it quickly,
  now it's gone!

Prayer

Thank you, Lord God, for the food we eat,
  for the people who grow it and gather it,
  for the people who make it ready for the shops,
  for cooks in many places:
    in our homes, in cafes, in schools and hotels;
and thank you, dear Lord, for the fun and pleasure we get from eating.
  Help us not to waste food,
  for there are many who have not got enough;
bless those who will go hungry today, and for many tomorrows,
  and teach men and women everywhere
    to share what they have with those who have nothing.

Bible stories: Sharing the harvest—Ruth 2.1-12
The wedding in Cana—John 2.1-10
Everyday pancakes (told in full)

Everyday pancakes

Danny's home did not have a front door—well, not a proper front door like all his friends' houses. You did not ring the bell and get let in and go through a hall to the other rooms. The door leading to Danny's home was nearly always open, specially in warm weather, and lots and lots of people were always walking in and out. You did not go into a neat hall, but into a large room full of tables and chairs. Danny had to squeeze past them and past a counter to get to a little door at the back of the room which led to his living room and the two bedrooms, the kitchen and the bathroom. There was a back entrance, too, but that was mostly used by people unloading vans and carrying through boxes of food.

Have you guessed? Danny lived in a little flat behind the small restaurant where his mother and father worked. They had a man called Pete who came in to serve at the tables with Father, because Mother could not do the cooking and serve the meals as well.

There was no other restaurant like it in town, and it was always busy. People came in for lunches and suppers from a long way away, because Mother's cooking was very special. All day, every day, she cooked pancakes for the people who came in to eat; and they were lovely. There were so many pancakes, or crepes as they were called, filled with delicious things like cheese, or ham, or mushrooms, or tomatoes, or even really special things like prawns or curried chicken. There were other pancakes for puddings, filled with jam, or bananas, or chocolate, and always served with a big dollop of cream on top.

At holiday times, Danny was allowed to watch his mother cooking the crepes. Beside her she had a huge bowl with the pancake mixture of flour, eggs and milk, ready to be cooked, and in front of her, instead of a gas stove, there was a huge flat circle of iron. Mother waited until this had been heated up, and was hot—very, very hot—then put her ladle into the pancake mixture and poured it onto the hot griddle. Quickly she spread it all over; it bubbled as it started to cook. Then Mother put a spoonful of cheese or mushrooms into the middle of the batter and waited until they were hot as well. When they were quite ready, she put her flat slicer under the top of the pancake circle and folded it over the filling, then she folded the bottom over the filling, and the two sides. It looked, thought Danny, like a thin brown paper parcel. Mother put a knob of butter right in the middle, slid the pancake onto a warm plate, and it was ready to be carried from the counter to the customer who had ordered it. Then she started all over again on the next one. Mother never seemed to get tired of making the crepes, and Danny never got tired of watching her make them.

When Danny was ten years old, he was told that he could help in the restaurant one lunch-time, but he must learn how to do it properly, and must always be very polite to the people who came in to order meals. For a few days Danny watched Pete, so that he would know exactly what to do.

'You can do some serving today,' Father said one morning. At twelve o'clock Danny was all ready, wearing a very clean shirt, and with his hands freshly scrubbed. A man and woman came in and sat down at a table for two. Danny picked up his little pad of paper and his pencil, and walked over to them. They were reading the menu, deciding what they would like inside their pancakes. Danny remembered to smile.

'Can I take your order?' he asked politely.

'I think I'd like a cheese filling,' said the woman.

'And I'll have ham and tomatoes in mine,' said the man.

One cheese, one ham and tomato, wrote Danny on his little pad of paper, and hoped Mother would be able to read it. He tore the paper off the pad, just as he had seen Pete do, and laid it on the counter so that Mother could see it. He fetched two knives and forks and paper napkins for the man and woman at *his* table, and made sure that they had salt and pepper, a water jug and two glasses. The restaurant was filling up, and Father and Pete were moving quickly in and out of the tables. Danny could hear pancakes sizzling on the griddle. Soon his would be ready. He had to fetch them as soon as they were cooked so that they would not get cold before they reached the customers.

He glanced over the room. *His* man and woman were talking together. He did hope he would not drop the plates, or tip a chair over on his way to them with the pancakes! Mother smiled at him over the counter, and nodded. That meant that one of the pancakes was ready.

'The cheese one is done,' she said, 'but be careful, the plate's hot.'

Danny picked up a cloth and held the plate with it. It was difficult to get across to his table as so many other people were now in the restaurant, but at last the plate was safely on the table. Danny went back to get the other plate and carried it across.

'Thank you,' said the man and the woman. 'And may we have some coffee?' asked the man.

Danny went to the coffee machine and poured hot coffee from the jug into two cups. Father had told him to take the coffee to the tables with a little jug of milk so that the people could put in just as much milk as they liked, and he must always make sure there was sugar on the table, and teaspoons in the saucers. What a lot to remember!

At last Danny's man and woman had finished, and the man called for the bill so that they could pay for the meal. Danny did ask if they wanted a sweet pancake first, but they said they did not have enough time.

Now Danny had to do some adding up! He was glad he had worked hard at arithmetic at school. He took the bill over to his father to make sure he had not made any mistakes, then he put it down on the table beside the man, just as Pete had shown him. The man and woman got up and walked to the desk by the door. The man gave the money for the meal to Father.

'What an excellent new waiter you have,' he said as he waited for his change, and he said it just loud enough for Danny to hear. 'I hope you pay him well!'

Father laughed. 'He's only doing it for today,' he said. 'He ought to learn while he's young. One day he might be manager here.'

The manager! Danny went quite red and smiled. He would work extra hard from now on. It was such fun making it Pancake Day for other people every day of the year!

A broken home

Project outline

Sadly, society today has a large proportion of broken homes. The causes of these need not concern us here but, as teachers, we see the effects clearly and too often. Withdrawal, aggression, lack of concentration, and numerous other reactions are symptoms of the tensions felt by young children living in an unhappy or broken home. Teachers having to cope with these behavioural problems may experience anger, sympathy, pity and helplessness towards the child and parents. As teachers, we must try to understand the child's needs so that our attitude to him or her is not influenced by our feelings towards the parents.

Some children feel they need to talk about a breakup at home; others keep painfully silent. Let those who want to share, do so; all they may need is a listening ear. If they will do this openly, it may help those who have deliberately kept silent.

The project leading to the Assembly will depend on your own class-room circumstances. Only you can judge the approach which will be of most help to the children. In some cases there will be no need for a project at all; the stories themselves, with a few appropriate words to link them with circumstances of which only you may be aware, will help many children listening.

The stories are simple ones, showing how animal families cope quite naturally with one or other parent taking care of the young. Some research by teacher and children will enable you to have pictures of 'one parent' family groups; here is a basic list to start you looking:

all cats; all bears; the gibbon (although family groups are common, father takes no part in the rearing); the anteater, kangaroo and wallaby; sparrows and budgerigars; and, more commonly for the class-room, guinea pigs, rabbits (but not the gerbil).

The Assembly

Hymns and songs

At half-past three	NCS 43, SSL 58
Come and let us sing	NCS 78
I'm very glad of God	SSL 22

Poem
My home
I can make my home a happy one,
    wherever it is;
and those who are in it happy too,
    with hugs and a kiss.

Home can be small, or a great big one,
    and those who are there
are trying their best to look after me
    by showing their care.

I can do lots by the way I give
    my help with a smile;
be with my home and my loved ones,
    dear God, all the while.

Prayer

We come from many homes, O God; please bless them all. Some of us are looked after by our mothers, some by our fathers, and some by both parents, or other people we love. Help our families, large or small, to be loving, and may we do our best to make them happy.

Stories

Bible story: Jesus blesses the children—Matthew 19.13-15
Father becomes Mother (told in full)
Mother Bear alone (told in full)

Father becomes Mother

Mortimer the Marmoset was extraordinarily proud of his home, for he and his mate, Maisie, had built it together. Maisie was expecting twins and spent a lot of time just lazing about in the nest, while Mortimer was out looking for food.

Mortimer and Maisie were about the size of squirrels, but were really related to the big family of monkeys. Both of them had grey silky coats and tiny monkey faces. What made them really handsome were the tufts of white hair which stood up round their ears. It was a shame that Maisie did not love Mortimer more. She thought he would make a good father, but she hoped he would leave her quite on her own once the babies were born. She did not really want to have much to do with them, and certainly did not want them running round her all the time. Mortimer, on the other hand, thought Maisie was fat and lazy; he wondered what she would do when she no longer had an excuse for lying there in the nest like an overfed fairy queen.

During one night, when the jungle trees were full of calling birds and strange sounds, Maisie's twins were born. Tiny little things, they looked exactly like their parents, except that their eyes were tight shut. Mortimer poked about in the nest to find them. He did not want fat Maisie lying on them by mistake! He nuzzled them until they moved and cried. Then he began to lick them clean. He looked at Maisie; she had gone straight to sleep, exhausted. He pushed the babies towards her, and they quickly found out how to drink her milk. Maisie did not even open her eyes, and after a bit the baby marmosets fell asleep.

In the morning, Mortimer found the twins awake, their eyes closed still, but already they were trying to peep out at the world. Mortimer backed up to them until they could feel him near.

It was strange how they seemed to know what to do, and Mortimer felt a very proud father indeed as they both scrambled onto his back, clinging on with their tiny feet.

'Hold tight, lads!' he squeaked as he wobbled along a branch of the tree. 'We'll take it easy today, then have a longer journey tomorrow.'

Maisie did not seem to notice that they had gone; she was still curled up in the nest. Mortimer supposed she would leave at some time to find herself food. He really could not bother with her, now that he was nursemaid to the twins.

He made a very good father, and the twins just loved riding round on his back. They got quite good at it, and Mortimer could scuttle along the branches knowing that they were quite safe. Of course, as time went by, they began to grow big and become heavy. Then he would leave one behind while he carried the other and left him in a safe spot while he dashed back again. Maisie never did care much for her babies; every now and again she glanced at them, and she fed them when they were hungry, but she would never make much of a mother. Much better to leave them both with Mortimer, who could care for them until they were old enough to leave home.

Mother Bear alone

Nothing could be seen for miles—nothing but white ice and snow. Now and again, if you looked really hard, you could see places where the ice ended and the sea began, but it was a grey sea, reflecting the grey-blue sky. Nothing moved, and there was no sound. In the far distance, Mrs Polar Bear was trundling into view, her thick coat only slightly more yellow than the surrounding snow. She was alone, and was looking for an ice cave where she could give birth to her baby. Mr Polar Bear had long since left her, and had gone off hunting seals on the far-off ice floes.

At last Mrs Polar Bear, who always called herself 'Patience', since no one else had given her a name, found what she was looking for. It was a tight little cave, deep and cosy. The ceiling, walls and floor were all of ice, and it was blue and dark, and very, very private. Patience lay down, for she was half asleep, and would not need to be fully awake for some time. One night, as she lay there, her little baby was born, tiny and quite helpless. Patience licked her all over, her huge tongue covering the baby bear cub.

'I shall call you Branca,' she said. 'My white, fair maiden.'

Branca only woke up to feed, and to snuggle closer into her mother's long white fur. Patience hardly felt her movements, but could see that Branca was growing day by day. It was a pity her father could not see her now. She told Branca about him, of his brave adventures, of the way he could run so quickly, in spite of his size, over the ice and snow, and how he could be still and silent for hours by an icehole, waiting to catch fish and seals.

'Will I ever see him or meet him?' Branca wanted to know.

'When he comes this way again, you will know him,' said Patience. 'He's the biggest polar bear for miles around. But he won't come back to live with us, little one. He is better by himself, roaming round and hunting for himself.'

'How will we manage, out there in that big white world?' asked Branca. She was getting bigger, her coat was longer and thicker, and her little round body was just longing to play outside the cave entrance. Patience knew it would soon be time to leave the safety of the cave. She would have to teach Branca so many things: how to look after herself when swimming in the cold water, how to catch fish, and how to find her way to the best seal grounds.

It was not easy for a mother alone, but Branca needed a mother to care for her, and Patience would never leave her until she was sure her daughter was old enough to find a mate and have her own babies.

The loss of a loved one

Project outline

It may be thought that bereavement is a subject too complex and too sensitive to be tackled with young children. This attitude seems to assume that they are not aware of death or, by silence, are protected from it. But it is often this very silence that leaves them totally unprotected, so that the death of someone known and dear to them can be the root cause of much more trauma and unhappiness than is normal or natural. To say that we can take away the sadness is unreal and false, but perhaps we can make it a little more bearable. Grief is a necessary part of acceptance and adjustment after bereavement, and we should not seek to take this away. But, by trying to look beyond the death, funeral, and immediate distress, we can help the child to see that life can become happy again, and that death does not necessarily mean total loss of a loved one.

As with the subject of broken homes, it is difficult to set out deliberately to construct a project round death. Some teachers may find that the death of a classroom pet will lead easily and naturally into a discussion on human death. Christian teachers may want to link the loss of a loved one with the promise of Christ: 'There are many rooms in my Father's house, and I am going to prepare a place for you. I would not tell you this if it were not so.' (John 14.2, GNB) Whether this promised 'place' is heaven as we have come to think of it, or a dimension known only to those who have passed into it, is not really the question at this point. What we are concerned with is the fact that when people die they are no longer with us, and we miss them. We are concerned with the feelings and attitudes of those left behind.

If the 'news' of some child includes the death of one of their family, or if some local or national tragedy has resulted in widespread coverage by the media, then an opportunity for this Assembly will arise. It is probably a mistake to force the subject; to do so might worry or frighten some children unnecessarily. If the topic of death has arisen, then the 'project' may consist only of a quiet, informal talk with your class. Try to encourage them to express their feelings about it, in words, pictures, in singing or in stories. This will help them not to bottle up feelings that are better dealt with in the open. You will probably encounter several different reactions: ones of sheer grief or of hopelessness, ones of anger and bitterness, confusion and frustration. Talk about them so that the children do not feel unnatural, wicked, or alone in their emotions.

It is important to leave the 'audience' after the Assembly in an atmosphere of hope, and of thankfulness for those who have died. To say that 'death is not the end' is a cliché expressed all too glibly. To say that the death of a loved one is not the end for those who have loved is far more relevant and meaningful.

The Assembly

Hymns and songs

When we're happy, full of fun	NCS 29
Praise him! Praise him!	NCS 79
When I needed a neighbour	SSL 35
Think, think on these things	SSL 38

Poem

When Grandma died

When I was told that Grandma had died,
I felt that she was gone,
and I remember how I cried
up in my room alone.

My Mummy wept, and Dad looked sad,
that never more would we
have Grandma bustling round our home
and drinking cups of tea.

We would not see her cheerful face
or hear her voice again,
and round our house, at the weekend,
we'd look for her in vain.

Then I felt black and angry
that Grandma left us so;
I felt that she'd been thoughtless,
and that she didn't know

how I would miss her visits.
I wished that I had said
how much I loved her stories,
when it was time for bed.

But I'll recall those stories,
and in my mind I'll hear
her lovely voice, remembering
when she was very near.

Music

Pavan for a Dead Infanta, Ravel
Praise to the Holiest in the Height from *The Dream of Gerontius*, Elgar
(The first is a slow and stately piece in which sadness is expressed; the second depicts the Angelic Choir singing the praises of God who has shown his love for the dead Gerontius, and is a thrilling climax of hope and thankfulness.)

Prayers

Dear Lord God, sometimes we feel very sad; please comfort us. Sometimes we feel angry and hurt, too, and we need comforting then. Help us to feel your love all round us, keeping us safe however we may be feeling.

Dear Lord, we feel sad today when we think of . . . When people die we miss them very much. Help us to be thankful for their lives, and to realise that soon we shall be happy again.

Stories

Bible story: Ruth—using selected verses: Ruth 1.1-8a, 14b-16,18,22; 2.1-3, 17-18a, 23; 3.1; 4.13-16

Grandpa's parting gift (told in full)

Grandpa's parting gift

Kenny loved cars. He had quite a collection of little model ones: a red Ford Escort, an elegant Mercedes, a silver Daimler, and many others. Mummy had allowed him to fix a big poster on his bedroom wall which had pictures of thirty different modern cars, and even some of the latest racing models. Kenny often went about making noises like a car, and sometimes he pretended to drive Daddy's Vauxhall, but of course he was too small to reach the pedals, and he had to strain his neck really hard to see out of the windscreen.

He always looked forward to Grandpa's visits with lots of excitement, because Grandpa drove a Triumph, and in good weather threw the roof back so that he could stick his arm straight up to wave to Kenny when he arrived. In Grandpa's car there was only room for two people, and the seats were low down, but it could zoom along really fast. When Kenny and Grandpa went out in it together it looked as if the trees and the houses were whizzing past, and Kenny loved the rush of air on his face, which pushed his hair back and made his eyes water.

When Grandpa came this Spring, however, he did not drive the Triumph. Instead, he rang Daddy and asked Daddy to fetch him.

'Has Grandpa's car broken down?' Kenny wanted to know.

'No, but Grandpa's a bit broken down himself,' said Daddy. 'He's not too well, and the doctor says he would get much too tired driving the car all this way.'

So this was not going to be much of a visit, thought Kenny to himself. Grandpa would have to sit about, resting, instead of taking Kenny for long exciting drives in his marvellous car.

A few days later, after Grandpa had settled himself in with the family, Kenny asked him about the Triumph. 'Is it still all right?' he asked. 'It hasn't been in an accident or anything, has it?'

'Oh, no,' said Grandpa. 'The car's fine. I sent it to the garage for a wash and polish the other day. Looks smashing now. Reminds me of the old Bugatti my father bought when I was a boy.'

'A Bugatti?' said Kenny. 'Was that a car?'

'Best car there ever was!' Grandpa said, and smiled as he thought back to when he was a small boy. 'They were fast and very noisy. We had a Type 55, I think.'

'What did it look like?' asked Kenny.

Grandpa took an old envelope from his pocket and began to draw with Kenny's pencil. 'It was low—like my Triumph,' he said, drawing a long bonnet and mudguards that curved right over the front wheels, along past the passenger seat and up over the back wheels. 'It had a narrow sheet of glass in front, which was the windscreen, but I don't remember a hood that pulled up; it was always quite open when I was given a ride in it. Just Dad and me, always. My mother said it was too noisy, and that Dad drove too fast. Anyway, there was only room for the driver and one passenger.'

By this time Grandpa had drawn the car. Kenny thought it looked fabulous. 'Could we build one?' he asked.

'Not if you mean a real one!' laughed Grandpa. 'But I tell you what—we could make a model one together!'

That sounded great, and Kenny spent the rest of that day collecting scrap things to make it from: an empty washing-up liquid container and tin foil, some huge old buttons his mother found for the wheels, and some bendy plastic strips that could be cut up to make the long mudguards. Kenny found scissors and glue and paint; he found some clear plastic for the windscreen, and Daddy gave him some shiny mirror screws for the headlamps.

They worked hard for the next day or two, Grandpa and Kenny. It was great fun, and Grandpa talked all the while, telling Kenny stories about Ettore Bugatti the Italian, who built the cars which were French, in a factory in Germany. The Bugatti belonging to Grandpa's father was made twenty-six years after Signor Bugatti had built his very first one in 1909. Most of Bugatti's cars were sports models or racers, Grandpa said, and they won more races than cars built by any other people at the time.

The model was finished the day before Grandpa had to go home. They had painted it bright blue, just like Grandpa's old car, with mudguards and the passenger seat in dark blue. It was the smartest model in Kenny's collection, even though it was home-made.

A few weeks later, Kenny heard that Grandpa had died. 'His heart wore out,' said Mummy, as she comforted Kenny.

At first Kenny was sad, and cried tears of unhappiness. Then he felt cross, and cried tears of anger. Grandpa was his best friend, and should not have died.

Kenny pushed the model Bugatti right to the back of his toy cupboard, so that he could forget Grandpa.

Grandpa was gone. In a few years he would have been forgotten. Kenny would never be able to tell all his school friends what a wonderful Grandpa he had, who took him for car rides, and could talk about old cars.

Three years later, when Kenny was at Junior school, his teacher asked everyone in the class to bring to school a favourite picture, or ornament, or book, to show the class and talk about. Kenny did not like many pictures, he did not have any ornaments, and he could not make up his mind about a favourite book.

'You've got your model cars,' said Daddy. 'Take one of those.'

Kenny's mind suddenly raced to think about what was at the back of his toy cupboard. 'Is Grandpa's model Bugatti an ornament?' he asked.

'Well, not at the moment,' said Daddy. 'I haven't seen it for years. Do you know where it is?'

Kenny rushed away to his bedroom, and to the toy cupboard. He tossed out some paints, a warship, two teddy bears, a pile of books, and four torn comics, before he came to the Bugatti. 'I'll take this,' he thought to himself, and found a box to carry it in. It reminded him of Grandpa: he could hear his voice so clearly and, when he shut his eyes, he could see Grandpa's face as he worked so hard to stick the parts of the model together.

'It's a Bugatti,' he said proudly, as he held up his model in class the next day.

'What's a Bugatti?' asked a boy in the front row, and Kenny suddenly remembered asking Grandpa the same question.

'A French car, designed and built by an Italian called Ettore Bugatti,' said Kenny; they were Grandpa's words. He went on to tell all the boys and girls all that Grandpa had told him.

So Grandpa, Kenny thought, lived on; Kenny was using his words, his very own words. Grandpa had not left him completely, because the things he had taught Kenny were still there: they had not gone. And they were valuable; they were like treasures that only he possessed, but which he could share with lots of other people.

Handicaps

Project outline

If you are fortunate enough to work in an area where children with handicaps can integrate, either fully or in part, with normal boys and girls, you may need to adapt this project. For some normal children, however, meeting people with either mental or physical handicaps can result in surprise, enquiry or, sadly, in some cases, in fear or revulsion. These last two reactions are nearly always caused by ignorance or apprehension about the unfamiliar and unknown. We can help to turn into concern and action whatever feelings children may have towards those who, through no fault of their own, are 'different'.

Spend time at the start of the topic looking at the normal differences between members of the class, eg, hair/eye colour; skin colour (even in an all white class); height, weight; hand spans; likes/dislikes etc. Make wall charts and pictures from the results. Point out that no two people, even twins, are exactly alike. Talk about differences in health, vision, tooth decay, and the number and variety of infectious illnesses the children have had. Help them to realise that everyone lives with handicaps to a certain extent, and that illnesses do occur, that no one is quite free from them.

Then the children will be ready to accept that some people have special difficulties of hearing, sight, movement, and so on. Talk about those handicaps that have been apparent since birth, also pointing out that some can be caused later by disease, illness or injury. Find out which are familiar to some of the children, like blindness, deafness, muscular dystrophy, diabetes, etc, and spend time talking about these, the signs of the disease by which they are recognised, the effect the illness or injury has upon movement, diet, etc. Let the children discover what particular difficulties they would encounter if they suffered similarly.

From mainly physical disorders move to mental disabilities. Many of these will be unknown, incomprehensible, and possibly frightening to small children, but many of them will have encountered children with Down's Syndrome disease, and may have someone suffering from it within their own families.

Just as our pupils are, for the greater part, children with no mental handicap, so Down's Syndrome victims are children with a mental disorder. We should not label them as 'Mongols' or even as 'Down's Syndrome' children. First and foremost they are *children;* that they happen to suffer from a mental illness is secondary.

As a climax to the topic, try to arrange to meet such boys and girls, and use the time in singing, playing games, using percussion instruments, watching a film or listening to a story. Meeting and mixing together will do more for understanding than any amount of talking; and doing something *with* the children, rather than *for* them, will lead to a pleasure out of which love and concern can grow.

The Assembly

Hymns and songs

For all the strength we have	NCS 30, SSL 16
Jesus' hands were kind hands	SSL 33
Look out for loneliness	SSL 36
O Jesus, we are well and strong	SSL 40

Poem (This should be read or recited by a different child for each verse, all coming together to say the last verse)

I'm alive!

I cannot hear the sounds you hear,
    for I am deaf, you see;
I do not know what music is;
    your voice unknown to me:
      but I'm alive, as you are too,
      I laugh, I love, and breathe like you.

I cannot see; the world is dark,
    sometimes a frightening place;
for I am blind; I do not know
    the smile upon your face:
      but I'm alive, as you are too,
      I laugh, I love, and breathe like you.

I cannot walk; my legs are weak;
    I'd like to run and play;
I wish that you would stay and talk,
    instead, you run away;
      for I'm alive, as you are too,
      I laugh, I love, and breathe like you.

74

I cannot think the way you do;
   I do not read or write;
I'm sometimes slow to speak and walk,
   I can't do sums quite right:
     but I'm alive, as you are too,
     I laugh, I love, and breathe like you.

And I am fortunate to be
   a healthy child, for I
can see, and hear, and run, and think;
   but from now on, I'll try
     in my good health to think of you,
     for I am laughing, loving, too.

So let's join hands, each helping each;
   a team of girls and boys;
let's go together through the world,
   and share our fears and joys:
     for we're alive, to laugh and love,
     all children of our God above.

Prayer

We thank you, dear Father, that you have made us all so different. Please give us kindness, and help us to understand those who are not like us, so that we may live together happily. Your world is big and beautiful, and you love us all so much.

Stories

Bible stories: Helping the helpless —Luke 9.37-43
                                      —Luke 5.18-20, 25

Different—yet alike (told in full)

Different—yet alike

Marcus had a letter in his pocket. He put his fingers over it, and wondered what to do about it. Mrs Hogarth, at school, had given a letter to everybody to take home for their mother or father. Marcus knew what the letter was about: it was an invitation to the school Christmas party, for all the pupils, and their Mums and Dads, and younger brothers and sisters.

'The school is like a big, happy family,' Mrs Hogarth had said, 'and we want to make it bigger still for this Christmas party. We've got plenty of room, so ask all your family along. We'll make them all welcome.'

'My brother will come,' Marcus's friend Tommy told him. 'He'll be five in March, so he's starting school after Christmas. It'll be great to let him see it all at the party.'

But Marcus was worried. He did not want his little sister at the party. She would not be coming to his school later anyway, because she went to another one already, a school with other children like her. Cheryl was slow to learn, and did not talk well, and might never be able to read properly. Marcus was used to her funny ways: the noises she made, the sloppy way she ate, dribbling the food from her mouth. But he did not want his friends staring at her and laughing. She would be the odd one out at the party, and it would be spoiled for him.

He handed the invitation to his mother. 'But you don't really need to come,' he said.

'Oh Marcus, you know we'd love to come,' said his mother, 'and it would be nice for Cheryl to see all your friends; you never bring any of them home.'

Of course he didn't, Marcus thought; his friends did not have sisters like Cheryl.

Marcus loved this time of day, when he was alone with Mother. Cheryl was brought home from her special school by a coach about an hour later. But even now, at this time, he just could not tell Mum that he did not want Cheryl at his school's Christmas party. She was so different from all the boys and girls there. He knew she was handicapped—that she would never be the same as they were. He loved her, just as Mum and Dad did, and he did not mind her playing with his toys at home, or making loud shouting noises, and laughing in a silly way, but he was sure his friends would point at her, and at him, and call her 'Marcus's funny sister'.

Mum cuddled Marcus. She understood how he felt, and he was glad. Then they heard the coach outside in the road, and Mother went to help Cheryl get off and come indoors. Marcus watched through the window. Cheryl waved at her friends, who grinned back at her, their fat little hands pressed to the coach windows. Cheryl carried in a letter, and Mother opened it, while Marcus undid Cheryl's coat buttons.

'Why, there's to be a party at Cheryl's school, and we're invited to it!' said Mother. 'But it's on the same day as your Christmas party, Marcus. Whatever shall we do?'

'Mine! Mine!' shouted Cheryl, jumping up and down.

Marcus was just going to say that *his* invitation had arrived first, when he suddenly stopped. This might be a way out of having to take Cheryl along to his school.

'Let's go to Cheryl's party,' he said.

Mother looked at him, then put her arm round him, as if to let him know she knew just what he was thinking. 'I think that's a lovely idea,' she said, and wrote a letter to Mrs Hogarth to explain why they would not be there.

A week later, Dad came home from work early, and drove Mum and Marcus and Cheryl to Cheryl's school. Cheryl was dressed in a smart red dress and new white socks and shoes. She was excited. 'Party! Party!' she kept saying, and grabbed Marcus by the hand as the car stopped in the car park.

The school hall had been decorated with balloons, streamers and paper chains, and there was coloured paper tied round the lights to make the room look warm and party-like. Mothers and fathers were sitting round the edge of the room, and the boys and girls like Cheryl were all in the middle round a teacher. She looked over and smiled. 'Come along, Cheryl,' she called. Cheryl left her coat with Mother and hurried to the middle of the floor. All the boys and girls with the teacher looked over at Marcus with big round eyes and open mouths. They were staring at him, and one boy pointed at him with a big grin on his face.

Marcus wanted to walk out again. He felt the odd one out. He did not like feeling different.

Soon the party was going well. The children at the special school played the same games as Marcus's friends would be playing, at that very minute, in his own school hall. True, some of the children could not move so quickly, and the teacher needed to give her instructions about the games in very simple words, but what they were doing was the same, even if some of the boys and girls needed help in walking, or someone to move them in the right direction.

'Now ask your brothers and sisters to join in the next game,' said the teacher.

Cheryl moved over to the corner where Marcus was trying to be invisible, and pulled at him with her hands. 'Game,' she said.

They are so happy, thought Marcus; they are all laughing and shouting, just like us at my school. It made him want to laugh and shout too. He had felt really different when he came in, but he did not notice it so much now, because everyone was so friendly.

Suddenly he realised that that was just how Cheryl would have felt at his school—the odd one out, and different. But everyone was friendly there, too, and Cheryl would have been made to feel at home, he was sure, as the boys and girls asked her to join in. They would probably have helped her, petted her, made a fuss of her. Marcus would have smiled and been proud of her.

The next day at school he spoke to his friend Tommy. 'Mum says she'll ask your mother if you can come to tea tomorrow. I want you to meet my little sister. She's great!'

Spring-cleaning

Project outline

Perhaps spring-cleaning is now out of date: modern appliances have done away with the need for the thorough annual scrub-down, which has been replaced by constant and fingertip cleanliness unknown to our grandparents. Yet the word 'spring-clean' remains in our vocabulary, conjuring up visions of tidying little-used cupboards, and wiping away accumulated dirt from inaccesible heights and depths. Spring is an eye-opening season. Outside, things are newly washed by the April rain and in the clear light of a fresh spring day our houses can seem dull and dusty.

Three approaches to topics on the subject of spring-cleaning are given.

Washing Mother's washing day—observation and recall of what is done. The clothes are probably sorted, by colour and/or fabric. Scraps of material which usually accumulate in a class-room could be sorted in this way too. For washing, the clothes are then piled into a washing-machine and powder added. Older children could discover more about detergents, and experiment with comparing the foam produced, the weight and texture of small amounts of the powder etc. Most children will be familiar with washing-machines, and may be interested in how washing was done in earlier times, and is still done in some places today.

Washing ourselves Why do we need soap? What is it, and where does it come from? Why do we need to wash? And what would happen if we did not wash? Simple principles of hygiene could be talked about, and enlarged upon; cleaning teeth, nails, hair—what we use and how we do it. The various implements for washing could be collected and displayed and discussed, then drawn or modelled. Include tooth-brushes, hairbrushes and combs, face-cloths, sponges, nail files. Other forms of soap or its alternatives could be brought into the class-room and talked about, eg, shampoo, washing-up liquid, shower gel, soap-flakes, etc.

Clearing and cleaning Centre this topic round the class-room itself. Why do we need to keep things tidy? Let the children find out the benefits of order and neatness by having a large pile of objects on the floor, placed in a confusing mass,

78

and asking the children to find a particular article. Make a game of this. Then rearrange the pile, grouping the objects either by size, use or colour, and let the children see how much easier selecting the correct article becomes. Later, give small groups other piles of things to sort—a large box of buttons could be sorted by colour into smaller containers, beads sorted into size or shape, or books into sets or subjects. If you can bear it, let the children turn out the various class-room cupboards, boxes and shelves. Make sure that they also see the necessity for wiping down the shelves, for dusting the cupboards, and for repairing or renewing boxes and other containers. Then the contents should be put back neatly, and in some sort of order.

After any of these topics, talk about spring-cleaning. Some of the boys and girls will have noticed evidence of this at home or in their grandparents' houses. Cleaning in preparation for house-painting, inside or out, may be going on too. Point out that cleaning is always done for good reasons of hygiene, comfort or convenience, and that at this time of year, in the fresh light of spring, we notice the dirt, we are ready for change, and we are spurred on by renewed energy.

The Assembly

Hymns and songs

For the beauty of the earth	NCS 89
This is a lovely world	SSL 8
I love the sun	SSL 12
All the flowers are waking	SSL 48

Poem

Spring-clean

Brush and scrub, sweep and sort,
   clean and wash and clear;
this is what we want to do
   at this time of year.

Spring is here with newness,
   trees all scrubbed by rain,
fields are washed to greenness,
   skies are blue again.

Empty out your corners,
    tidy out your drawers,
take a dustpan to the shelves,
    scrub the dusty floors.

Spring again, start again,
    everything looks new,
inside, outside, all is fresh,
    spring-cleaned through and through.

Music

First Movement from *Symphony No 1 (Spring)*, Schumann
(For sheer effervescence and busy-ness of spring-cleaning and life)

Prayer

Dear God, your world looks beautiful today, and we are glad to be alive in it. Thank you for the rain, washing clean the pavements, and for the sun and wind, which blow-dry the trees and grass. Help us to make your world tidy, and keep it tidy, so that everyone can enjoy it and be happy in it.

Stories

Bible story: The lady who looked after Elisha—2 Kings 4.8-10
The rooks spring-clean (told in full)

The rooks spring-clean

'Caw caw! Caw caw!' Father Rook was calling. He flew in wide circles, knowing that Mother Rook would not be far away. His loud cry brought lots of other rooks hurrying to the colony, the huge family who lived in the tree-tops by the farmyard. Father Rook settled on a branch and fluffed up his glossy black feathers. The sun was shining again after days of rain and wind, and he knew it was time to be looking for a nest. Some rooks had already found theirs, and stood guard over them, daring anyone else to try to claim them.

Mother Rook wheeled nearby at last. 'Where is it? Where is it?' she called. Some years they found the same nest that had been theirs last spring. The nests were always there, even in the winter when they smudged the bare branches of the elm trees like a scattering of ink-blots. Always the same farmer's field, and always the same group of high trees, year after year.

The noise of the gathering rooks was very loud. Down below the farmer looked up and smiled. 'Rookery's busy again,' he said to his sheep-dog as they went on their way to the lambing-folds. Father Rook balanced his feathered legs on one of the branches, while Mother Rook inspected the nest built between the strong twigs near the top of the tree. 'This is the one,' she cawed. But the old nest had been rather torn by the winter winds, and seemed thin and bare.

'It will need repairing and cleaning,' remarked Father Rook with a sidelong glance at it.

'More twigs, more twigs,' Mother Rook called as he flew off. She must get the nest rebuilt, adding sticks and mud to make it strong, and then they must line it with soft spring grass, hair from the farmyard, and perhaps with warm wool left behind by the farmer's sheep.

'Out you go!' she said to a rotting twig, lifting it over the side of the nest with her beak. In a few days' time, when she laid her eggs, they would need to be kept warm and dry, and the nest would need to be safe and comfortable for the young birds that would hatch from the eggs. Father Rook rushed backwards and forwards with sticks and twigs and Mother Rook arranged each one carefully and neatly, knowing just where they should go. Sometimes one of the other rooks flew too close, trying to steal one of her twigs. Mother Rook flapped her wings at the intruder, and scolded him loudly. 'Get your own! Get your own!' she cawed.

Those next few days in March were very busy ones. The nest was cleared, cleaned, tidied and turned out. Both Mother and Father Rook came and went, twigs in their beaks, until the old nest looked like new. Then they swooped to the hedges and fences, carrying off all the fluff, feathers and wool that they could find, to push into all the draughty cracks and over the sharp ends of the sticks.

Then Mother Rook settled herself into the comfy home, fidgeting and nudging until the shape and size was just right for her body. Her spring-cleaning was over. The eggs could now be laid, and she would keep them warm and safe until they hatched. And Mother Rook knew that Father Rook was busy somewhere, looking for a tasty grub or two to bring home for her supper.

At Easter time

Project outline

With the cry 'He is risen!' ringing round the world on Easter Day, our spirits are lifted with the hopes of better things to come for all people. But hope is empty without action. We cannot just sit back in anticipation, believing that the nations of the world will suddenly negotiate for peace; that deprivation, starvation and unemployment will miraculously disappear; and that all men will thereafter live with dignity, self-respect and concern for each other. What we do now, in a seemingly ineffectual and insignificant way, could be the beginnings of a better world. Christian teachers, those passing on the Easter message of hope and new beginnings, must be aware that the responsibility on them is great: to sow the seeds for a new world that the boys and girls, their children, and their children's children, can inherit.

'Then he who sat on the throne said, "Behold! I am making all things new!" ' (Revelation 21.5, NEB) This is the suggested theme for the Easter Assembly. Easter did not become associated with springtime by accident. Jesus was crucified at the time of the Jewish Feast of the Passover, the spring festival. Remembering his resurrection, it was natural for Christians to celebrate it as new life in Jesus, and in the natural world waking after winter. The word Easter derives from the name of the pagan goddess of spring—Eostre.

The Easter Assembly will most likely take place a little while before Easter Day, and the story is therefore set in the days leading up to it, when hope is high, and the expectation of holidays, presents and Easter eggs is on the children's minds.

As you work preparing Easter cards or presents, your topic will already be on its way. Supplement all you are doing with the biblical story of Easter (told simply), and of the new beginnings offered to the disciples with the resurrection. Have examples of the new beginnings of spring: twigs with swelling buds, spring flowers, tadpoles in a jar, pictures of chrysalises, etc. Use a tape with the sounds of lambs, birdsong, or Easter carols. Have a table display at the Assembly with a colourful inscription saying 'New Life at Easter!' Learn and sing a verse of a little-known Easter carol, or present a simple enactment or mime of Matthew 28.1-8, conveying the excitement felt by the women as they ran to tell the disciples their news.

The Assembly

Hymns and songs

Seeds and bulbs are all asleep	NCS 16
At Easter time the lilies fair	NCS 69
Morning has broken	SSL 3
All the flowers are waking	SSL 48

Poem

Time of gladness

As the buds burst into blossom
  after early rain,
we can leave behind our troubles,
  we can start again.

Easter is a time of gladness,
  all things being new;
Jesus, all our fresh beginnings
  we will bring to you.

Music

Overture: Land of the Mountain and the Flood, MacCunn
(A modern overture which sounds exciting)

Prayer

Thank you, Lord Jesus, for your life.
Thank you, Lord Jesus, for your love.
Thank you, Lord Jesus, for the new life which comes at Easter time.

Stories

Bible stories: Mary's happiness—Matthew 28.1-8
              Song of Spring—Song of Songs 2.11-13a
New beginnings (told in full)

New beginnings

'I want to go to the swings,' said Lizzy, eating her lunch.

'Not this afternoon,' said Grandma. 'Mrs Mills wants us to do some shopping for her, and we won't be going near the swings.'

'Can I buy an ice cream?' asked Lizzy.

'It's far too cold for ice creams!' said Grandma as she cleared away the dishes. 'Come and help in the kitchen, there's a good girl.'

Lizzy did not feel like being a good girl, and she certainly did not feel like helping Grandma wash the dishes.

'I broke a plate last time,' she said.

'Then you can feed the cats while I do the washing-up,' said Grandma.

Lizzy felt cross. Grandma was always stopping her doing the things she wanted to do, or finding other jobs for her. It was not fair. If Mummy was here she could do just as she liked. Well, perhaps not, but Lizzy was sure Mummy was better than Grandma at saying 'Yes', or at finding really nice things to do. But Mummy had gone to hospital and Grandma had come over to look after Lizzy and Daddy.

'I wish Mummy was here,' said Lizzy, rather unkindly.

'She'll be home soon,' said Grandma, who was not enjoying looking after Lizzy and all her grumbles.

It was near Easter, and Lizzy had seen an Easter egg that she would like. It was huge, and had pink silver paper wrapping and a beautiful pink bow on the front. Grandma said it was much too big for a little girl, and cost too much money.

It was raining when they started out for the shops, so Lizzy had to wear her wellington boots, which were too small; and her woolly gloves, which were too big. Grandma said they had to hurry to catch the bus, but Lizzy dawdled, looking at the rain splashing into the gutter, and the bus came round the corner while Grandma was telling her to hurry up. They had to run the last few yards, and the bus driver looked annoyed that they had held up his busful of passengers.

The shops were crowded and Lizzy was cold. She hated shopping. She wandered away to look again at the chocolate eggs, and she heard Grandma calling.

'Lizzy! Lizzy, where are you?' Lizzy kept quiet. She did not want Grandma to find her, just so that they could go and choose woolly bedsocks for Mrs Mills. Grandma came bustling round into the chocolate department, looking very cross.

'Oh, Lizzy, you are a naughty girl!' she grumbled. 'You must stay close to me. I can't go round looking for you everywhere!'

'I wish Mummy was here!' said Lizzy again, only quietly now, so that Grandma could not hear. She wanted to say, 'I don't like Grandma!' very loudly, so that everyone in the shop would hear; but she didn't.

That evening, after Daddy had visited Mummy in hospital, he had some good news to tell Grandma and Lizzy. 'Mummy will be home before Easter!' he said.

Lizzy looked so happy that Daddy had to go and make Grandma a cup of tea to stop her being too upset.

Grandma wanted Lizzy to go to the shops with her again the next day. She had to fill up the larder, she said, so that Mummy would not need to tire herself with a heavy load of shopping as soon as she came home from the hospital. It was a kind thing to do, but Lizzy did not want to do it with Grandma.

'Can I go and play with my friend?' she asked.

'No,' said Grandma.

'Can I stay here by myself, while you go to the shops?'

'No,' said Grandma.

Lizzy could not think what else she might do, so she hid in the airing cupboard. She could hear Grandma calling, but she did not answer.

'Where is that naughty girl?' grumbled Grandma, looking into Lizzy's bedroom, and in the bathroom. Lizzy kept very still, and was as quiet as a mouse.

Then she heard Grandma talking over the fence to Mrs Smithers who lived next door. 'I've got to catch that bus into town,' Grandma was saying. 'Lizzy's hiding somewhere, the bad girl. I wish you'd come in for a little while; I can't leave her all alone in the house.'

Then Lizzy heard Mrs Smithers coming to the front door, and she heard Grandma going out.

'Good!' thought Lizzy. 'Now I haven't got to do the beastly shopping with her.' After a few minutes she crept out of her hiding-place. Mrs Smithers was standing in the kitchen.

'Why, Lizzy, you did give me a start!' she said. 'Wherever have you been?'

'Hiding,' said Lizzy briefly. She was not going to tell where her hiding-place was, in case she needed to use it again.

'I think you're playing your Grandma up a bit,' said Mrs Smithers. 'You look like a thunder-cloud. What's up?'

Suddenly Lizzy burst into tears. She had not meant to, and surprised herself and Mrs Smithers. She knew she had been naughty, and cross, and silly, all the time Grandma had been staying, and she hoped Mrs Smithers would understand. She felt an arm go round her.

'Come on, chick, let's do something about it,' Mrs Smithers was saying. 'Let's make a lovely tea for Grandma. Let's cook some little cakes; you can put the cherries in.'

That sounded fun, and it sounded like a good way of showing Grandma that Lizzy was sorry.

'Easter should be such a happy time,' said Mrs Smithers, as she beat up butter and sugar and eggs. 'Wouldn't you like to make a fresh, happy start? I know you'll feel better when Mummy comes home, but wouldn't it be nicer to begin now? Grandma's had rather a difficult time with you, you know.'

Mrs Smithers was quite right. A new beginning was just right for Easter. Together they put flour and cherries into the cake mixture, then Lizzy helped Mrs Smithers put spoonfuls of it into little paper cases, which went into the oven to be baked.

'I'll get out the tray,' said Lizzy when Mrs Smithers was putting the kettle on a little later. It was really quite nice doing things together. Grandma must have felt quite lonely, having to do everything on her own.

When they heard Grandma's key in the front door, Lizzy rushed into the hall to meet her. 'I'll take your shopping bag,' said Lizzy, 'and we've got a surprise for you!' She led Grandma into the living room and made her sit down. Mrs Smithers came in with the tray. Lizzy beamed with pleasure as Grandma examined the little cherry cakes.

'Did you really make these for me?' she asked.

Lizzy chuckled, and passed her a paper napkin. 'I do love you, Grandma,' she whispered.

Lizzy felt so much happier. It was funny, she thought, how all the time when she had sat back and let Grandma do things for her, she had been miserable, and yet the moment she started to do things for Grandma, she felt really happy! And Mummy would be home tomorrow! They would all have a new start at Easter— what a lovely time it would be!

The sun and space

Project outline

There are many aspects for a project on space, but it would confuse and perhaps bore the children if you attempt to cover too much at once. Choose one subject, which may stimulate further interest and enquiry later on, from those given below. Your own research should fill out the areas you wish to emphasise and expand. Each topic gives ample opportunity for wall charts, friezes, collages, new vocabulary, counting and measuring, and other activities which could be used or displayed at the Assembly.

The sun   Begin this topic during sunny weather so the sun's heat and light can be fully appreciated. Point out how sunlight makes people feel good, and what good the sun can do by helping in growth cycles, providing light even when the sun is hidden behind dense clouds. Its heat is often intense. The sun is also a star (made up of hydrogen and helium), giving out a tremendous amount of energy which is absorbed by the earth. Hydrogen fuel from the sun has been burning for about 5,000 million years, and will probably go on for as many years again. Some other stars are bigger and brighter than our sun, but even so it is enormous compared with the Earth. If the children could begin to understand eclipses, give some information on them. Show pictures of the tropics, where the sun is directly overhead, and of arctic regions where the sun only shows during certain months of the year, and talk about the effect this has on vegetation, wildlife, humans, etc. Additional work could be done on the seasons: how and why they occur, their special features in this and other parts of the world. (Emphasise to the children that they should never look directly at the sun, as great damage could be done to their eyes.)

The solar system   The sun, as the centre of the solar system of which our earth is a small part, can again be the starting point for this topic. To help the children understand the movements of the planets round the sun, attach a ball or an orange to a piece of string, and let one of them swing it round and round. Explain that the hand holding the string is like the sun, and the string keeps the ball whirling, just as the sun's gravity keeps the planets whirling in orbit. Liken the planets to balls, moving round the sun, and reflecting its light. The other planets can be seen from

the earth, but are so far away they can only be seen as stars. Make charts or models to show the positions of the planets in the solar system. Most astronomers think that the solar system began as a cloud of gas and dust, the particles of which came together by gravity to form the sun. More parts of this cloud condensed to form the planets, together with dust and gas from other parts of space. Four thousand five hundred million years ago the sun was already shining and the planets had been formed.

How small we are   For very young children it may be enough to concentrate on where we are in space, doing a little work on each of the following areas before the Assembly: we are in our class-room; in our school; in our street; in our town/city/village; in our country; in the world (ie, the planet Earth); in the solar system; in a galaxy; in the universe.

Other topics before the Assembly could include: astronauts and space; moon landings; space shuttles; life on other worlds. The children would learn much by visiting an observatory or planetarium. Interest would also be stimulated by a visitor who could speak simply about astronomy, telescopes, etc.

The Assembly

Hymns and songs

What makes the daytime	NCS 20
Space-men are ready	NCS 39
We praise you for the sun	SSL 13
5 4 3 2 1 and zero	SSL 45

Poem

Daylight

How do we know there's a sun up there,
when the day is all gloomy and grey?
  Where is it hiding, where has it gone,
  when the rain falls in torrents all day?

Daylight is sunlight, even in rain,
and without it we'd live in the night;
   in darkness and cold God's world would die,
   for everything needs the sun's light.

Music
   Uranus from *The Planets Suite,* Holst

Prayer
   God's world by day is full of light,
   He made the sun, so brilliant bright,
   he set the moon to shine at night,
         God loved what he had done.
   So praise the Lord—clap hands and sing,
   let's shout our praise for everything,
   let all the world with voices ring,
         we love what God has done.
   Dear Lord, you made this world so fair,
   with warm sunlight and fine fresh air,
   may people praise you everywhere
         for all that you have done.

Stories
   Bible passages for adaptation: God's creation—Genesis 1.1–2.3
                             —Psalm 19.1-6
   Man finds out (told in full)

Man finds out

'We've been asked to call at the Priestleys' house today,' said Mama, as she sat with her two children at the breakfat-table. Anna and William looked at each other. They knew they would have to put on their best clothes and be on their best behaviour for the visit. The Reverend Joseph Priestley was an important man in their Yorkshire town.

That was long ago, and the clothes children wore in those days were often stiff and starchy, and not at all comfortable. Anna was afraid they would have to sit very still, and they would not be allowed to talk together, or giggle.

At three o'clock sharp they climbed into their black carriage and set off. The sun was bright and hot, and as they arrived William looked longingly at Mr Priestley's garden with its exciting little paths and high green hedges. He wished he could play hide-and-seek there instead of going into the house to make polite conversation in the drawing-room!

Mr Priestley was at the door to greet them. *He* was not all dressed up for a tea-party, thought William, looking at the vicar's shirt-sleeves and black waistcoat. 'Come in, come in!' said Mr Priestley warmly. 'I'm doing an experiment; you youngsters might like to watch.'

While Mama followed Mrs Priestley into the drawing-room, Anna and William were taken into Mr Priestley's library. There were books everywhere, but also glass jars and bottles, measuring-sticks, pens and notebooks. What could Mr Priestley be doing?

'Come and look at this,' said the vicar, showing the children a little wire cage. 'It's a mouse!' said William. 'Look, Anna, a mouse!'

Anna liked mice; Mother said it was not ladylike to like mice. She leant down to poke her fingers through the wire bars. 'What's he there for?' she asked.

'He helps in my experiments, ' said Mr Priestley with a twinkle in his eye. 'I am just going to try something. Would you like to watch?'

The Reverend Priestley first led them through the garden door out into the warm sunshine, then down to the neat kitchen garden. 'Pick me one or two bits of mint, if you will,' he asked William. 'Then we'll take them indoors and use them in my experiment.'

William picked the sweet-smelling mint and wondered what they could be going to do with it. 'Does the mouse help with this experiment?' he asked.

'You wait and see!' the vicar replied as they went indoors. He took a large glass jar from a table and put it on a shelf in a dark corner of the room. 'Put the mint into the jar,' he told William. Mr Priestley went to the cage where the mouse was. Very gently he lifted it out and put it into the jar with the mint leaves. He covered the jar so that no air could get in or out. The little grey mouse sniffed round the bottom of the jar, then stood on his back legs and tried to climb up the glass sides, but it was much too slippery for him. Anna laughed as he tried again and again, then ran round the bottom of the jar, his little nose quivering and his whiskers shaking.

They all watched the little mouse. He stopped running round to stare at them through the glass, then scuttled off round to the other side. Soon he began to get slower, and seemed a little sleepy.

'Does he want a nap?' asked Anna. 'He's just sitting there now.'

'I don't think so,' said Mr Priestley, thoughtfully. 'You see, the air in the jar is getting all used up as the mouse breathes it in. You couldn't breathe for long in a glass jar, could you?'

William and Anna were a bit worried. Would the mouse die because it could not breathe? Surely Mr Priestley would not allow that to happen!

'Let's see what happens if I move the jar,' said the vicar, and carried it over to the window sill. He pushed the heavy curtains back as far as they would go, and the children blinked in the brilliant sunlight. They could feel its warmth coming into the room.

As they watched the little grey mouse, he began to move about a bit. His eyes looked brighter, and he stood up on his back legs again to try to climb the sides of the glass jar. William felt the top of the jar. It was still firmly in place. No air was getting in from the outside, so how had the mouse got enough air to start breathing again?

'It must be something to do with the mint, I think,' said William.

'And something to do with the sunshine,' said Anna.

Mr Priestley was smiling. He looked very pleased with himself. 'Today we have discovered something really important,' he told the children. 'The sunlight, shining on the mint leaves, has allowed air to be given out by the leaves into the jar, and it is this air that the mouse is now breathing! Any leaves would have done the same.' Carefully Mr Priestley took the mouse out of the jar and put it back into the wire cage. 'Let's go and tell the ladies!' he said.

The three of them burst into Mrs Priestley's quiet drawing-room.

'Where have you been, Joseph?' she asked. 'Aren't you going to allow these children to eat their tea and cakes?'

William and Anna tucked into the little biscuits and the honey cakes, and listened while Mr Priestley explained about the experiment.

'I just knew that God must have made everything for a purpose,' he said. 'Birds, animals, plants, and people—they all have their part to play upon this earth. Now we have discovered that animals cannot live without plants, and plants cannot live without sunshine. How good God is!'

After tea Anna and William were allowed to walk in the garden. The house had been cool, but outside the sun was warm and bright.

'We love the sun, too,' said Anna.

'I don't think I could live without it!' said William, as he tilted his head to feel the warmth on his face.

'How good God is!' they said together.

(The story is based on the knowledge of an experiment by the Revd Joseph Priestley in 1771. At that time oxygen was an unknown gas, identified after further experiments by Priestley in 1774. Photosynthesis was not discovered until fairly modern times.)

Giants of yesterday and today

Project outline

Giants are familiar fictional characters to children. Huge, magical, mythical creatures, they are usually depicted as bad or menacing, striding across the landscape or inhabiting castles that can only be entered by intrepid adventurers. In folklore they have been blamed for falls of rock, volcanic upheavals, violent storms and floods. And yet they have a fascination for children matched only by that of dinosaurs, and teachers and parents can tell tales of these awesome characters sure of a wide-eyed and instant response. This project will deal not only with fictional giants; it will also include giants of the animal and plant world, and humans who have shown gigantic qualities of bravery, kindness and service to mankind.

Begin by reading or telling one or two stories about fictional giants: *Jack and the Beanstalk,* or *The Little Tailor,* or a simplified version of *Lilliput.* Encourage the children to draw, dramatise or write about the stories, and keep all work that can be shown at the Assembly.

Bible stories of David and Goliath, and the lesser-known one of David being saved from the giant Ishbibenob, could be included.

The children will be interested in stories of the Giant's Causeway in Northern Ireland; include also information about other gigantic natural formations, eg, Mount Everest, Sahara Desert, Pacific Ocean. Listen to some music which has vast connotations, eg, *The Planets Suite,* Holst.

Move on to giants in the animal world. Have pictures of giraffes, the tallest land animals; elephants, the heaviest; the blue whale, which is even heavier but which lives in the sea; gorillas, largest primates; St Bernard dogs, the biggest dogs; ostrich, largest bird, etc. Be prepared with information about the giant panda and the giant toad, which are both giants in name. Dinosaurs could be mentioned here.

In the plant kingdom, use pictures of the giant sequoia trees of California; of white water lilies *(Nymphaea alba),* the largest blooms found in Great Britain; also giant sunflowers. Show illustrations of the huge cacti in New Mexico, and the tall cabbbage plants grown in the Channel Islands.

The boys and girls could make drawings of all these things, perhaps measuring out some of their dimensions in the playground or against the school buildings.

Towards the time of the Assembly introduce the rather abstract idea that even if people are not as big as giants, their qualities of leadership or goodness can sometimes become gigantic in comparison with other people's. Find newspaper or magazine articles which tell of bravery, endurance, generosity, etc, and discuss them with the children.

The Assembly

Hymns and songs

Praise be to God for the wind that blows	NCS 2
God made the world. He made the moon and sun	NCS 3
When a knight won his spurs	SSL 34

Poem

I can be a giant

Are you tall as a house?
No, neither am I.
Can you reach up to the stars
in the dark night sky?

Can you step over a lake,
or pull up a tree?
Can you count all the sparrows
or weigh all the sea?

Are you brave as a lion,
or strong as a bear?
Can you fly like an eagle,
or run like a hare?

Things like these are for giants,
not people at all;
just thinking about them
can make me feel small!

But I can be quite big
in things that I do—
be a giant of kindness:
and so, too, can you!

Music

Toccata from *Organ Symphony No 5,* Widor
(This piece gives the effect of heaviness)

Prayer

Lord of the wide world,
of things big and small,
please listen; and bless us,
and be with us all.

Stories

Bible stories: David and Goliath—1 Samuel 17.20-51
David and Ishbibenob—2 Samuel 21.15-17
Jasmine the giant (told in full)

Jasmine the giant

Jasmine's brother Ali had just learnt to swim. She was proud of him, because no one else in the family could swim: not Father, not Mother, and not even Jasmine's bigger brother, Ibrahim, who was twelve. Ali, who was nine, had learnt with his class at school; Jasmine wanted him to teach her how to swim, but Mother said she was too small; she would sink, even in the shallow end at the swimming-baths! Ali, of course, liked to show off. He was always teasing Ibrahim: 'I can swim. You can't!' he would say, and Ibrahim would walk out of the room. He knew there were things that he could do that Ali had not learnt to do yet, but it would not do much good to keep pointing that out.

'One day I'll be able to swim, too,' Ibrahim said to himself. He had watched Ali in the swimming-baths, and practised moving his arms and legs, just as if he was swimming, while lying on the bedroom floor. If he knew how to do that, then swimming would be quite simple, he thought, when he got in the water.

One fine summer day Ibrahim packed his swimming trunks into a carrier-bag, with a big blue towel. He put his head round the kitchen door and said, 'I'm going out now.'

His mother looked up. 'Oh, Ibrahim,' she said. 'If you're going near the shops, please bring me back some rice. And take Jasmine with you. She doesn't know what to play with, and I'm very busy.'

Ibrahim had not expected this. He did not need to go near the shops to get to the river, and he certainly did not want to drag Jasmine, who was only six, round with him all the morning. He opened his mouth to say so, but Mother had put the money for the rice on the table, and had turned her back. He supposed they could run to the shops first, then on to the river, and he could have a quick bathe before they both went back for lunch.

'Do I *have* to take Jasmine?' he asked.

'Oh, please do, Ibrahim,' said Mother. 'She's right under my feet; besides, she needs some fresh air.'

'Come on, then, girl,' said Ibrahim roughly. He thought perhaps Jasmine might be useful—she could carry the rice.

'What's in your bag?' asked Jasmine as they walked to the shops.

'Nothing,' said Ibrahim.

'It can't be nothing,' said Jasmine, 'because I can see something.'

'Don't ask questions,' said Ibrahim. He did not want to talk.

When they had bought the rice, Jasmine asked if she could have an iced lolly. 'I'm hot!' she said.

'No, I'm not buying one,' said Ibrahim, and walked off very quickly in the direction of the river.

'This isn't the way home,' said Jasmine, catching him up. She knew that the little alley-way led to the path beside the river.

'I'm just going for a swim, if you must know,' said Ibrahim. 'You can look after my clothes if you like.'

'But you *can't* swim!' said Jasmine.

'Well, neither can you, baby,' said Ibrahim crossly. 'At least I know the strokes.'

Behind a bush, Ibrahim put on his swimming trunks. Jasmine thought how strong he looked, his brown body firm, and his black hair shining in the sun. She sat down by his towel, and put the rice inside the empty carrier-bag. It was hot in the sun, so she moved into the shade of one of the bushes. A low branch had been broken off, and she used it to pull Ibrahim's clothes nearer to her.

'Is it cold?' she asked, as Ibrahim felt the water with his toe.

'Not very,' said Ibrahim, but he'd already begun to shiver; the very thought of all that water in front of him was enough to make him change his mind about wanting to swim! But if Ali could do it, so could he. He walked on into the water through the mud, not looking back, in case Jasmine should see how nervous he was.

Suddenly the mud floor beneath him sloped down sharply, and Ibrahim gasped as the water came up to his waist. It really was cold. He held his arms up out of the water while he thought of the swimming strokes he had practised. He went another two steps, and was suddenly in deep, moving water. He thrashed his arms and kicked his legs, but he was frightened, and could not remember how to stay afloat.

Jasmine watched, fascinated. If that was swimming, it did not look like Ali's swimming; he always went quite smoothly through the water. Ibrahim's head disappeared as he lost his footing. Jasmine supposed he was diving; how clever he was to know how to do it! But when his head came up again, he was spluttering and waving his arms about.

'Are you all right?' shouted Jasmine, but Ibrahim could not answer before his head disappeared again. Suddenly Jasmine realised he was not swimming at all—he was drowning! But she could not swim, so she could not go in to save him. She started to shout and cry. She ran to the edge of the water. Ibrahim was not far away, but the river looked very deep just where he was. She was still holding the long stick from the bush. It would reach Ibrahim if she leant forward carefully.

'Here, hold this!' she shouted, as Ibrahim splashed about in a frightening way.

'Ibrahim! Take the end of my stick!'

Somehow, Ibrahim's arm touched the stick, and he grabbed it with such force that Jasmine was nearly dragged into the water with him. But her foot was right against a big stone, and she did not topple forward. She held the stick with both hands as tightly as she could, while Ibrahim, his head above water now, held on to the other end. For some time they stayed like that. Jasmine was not strong enough to pull her brother back to the river bank, and Ibrahim was too tired to struggle back himself.

Just when Jasmine thought she could not hold on any longer, she heard someone coming along the river path. It was a man pushing a bicycle. He took one look at the two children then rushed to help them. Leaning forward as far as he could, the man was able to reach Ibrahim's hand, and pulled him out of the water.

Ibrahim was so exhausted that he lay quite still, but Jasmine could see that he was all right. He coughed and spluttered, then sat up. Jasmine burst into tears. The man fetched Ibrahim's towel, and wrapped it round the boy's shivering shoulders.

'I'll take you two home,' he said, and asked where they lived. He lifted Jasmine onto the bicycle saddle, and pushed her along, while Ibrahim was made to run beside them to get himself warm again.

You can imagine what happened when they got home! There was such a to-do! Mother cried and hugged the two children, Father thanked the kind man who had brought them both home, while Ali ran round them all, promising to teach anyone to swim, just in case it happened again.

When Ibrahim's teeth had stopped chattering, and he had changed into dry clothes, he was able to tell them exactly what had happened, and how silly he had been to think he could go swimming on his own.

'If it hadn't been for Jasmine and her long stick, I should have drowned,' he said.

Jasmine was hugged and kissed and given ice cream to eat. She was a heroine!

Later a man came to the house to ask about the whole story. He wanted to write about it for his newspaper, and take a photograph of the little girl who had saved her brother's life.

'You're not very big,' said the man to Jasmine, 'but what you did was a giant act of bravery! Everyone is proud of you.'

Jasmine smiled. All she wanted to do was to learn to swim!

Jealousy

Project outline

Jealousy is a common emotion for young children to experience. Most parents are on the look-out for jealousy in the existing child or children when a baby brother or sister is born. It cannot always be avoided or dealt with satisfactorily, but when problems caused by it arise they can be quite easily identified. Not so easy to be forewarned about is the jealousy felt by a middle child towards his or her siblings. This short project is concerned with both types of jealousy, but the story is about a child who is envious of both his older brother and baby sister. It must not be assumed that jealousy is found only in childhood, although much of the adult emotion stems from an early age.

In class, notice the reactions of the child whose mother has recently given birth to a new baby. Does he feel 'dethroned' or rejected? Is he unwilling to talk about the new baby? Does his behaviour change so that he now shows signs of aggression, or of constantly seeking attention? These reactions may not become obvious for several weeks, by which time his parents may be neglecting the special attention he was given at the time of the baby's birth. It may help for the child to be frank about his real feelings, or to express them in drawing, acting, or physical activity. If you think so, ensure that the rest of the class, or at least a large group from it, is engaged on the same activity so that the child in question is not singled out.

More difficult to identify is the jealousy of a younger child for an older one, particularly if he is at the same time experiencing the normal reaction against a new brother or sister. A middle child may feel somewhat insignificant: not old enough to have the privileges of an older child, and not young enough to warrant the full attention of his parents.

As a group, Middle School Infants often feel somehow deprived. They look back with longing to their reception year unaware that much of the play in which they freely indulged was an important introduction to all learning skills. They look forward to the time when they will have certain privileges. Take them through one or two of their early games and let them play again with some of the simple toys of the reception class. Discuss with them what they were actually learning through this play: skills, both social and individual, that helped them to mature in readiness for the new experiences of their second year. Next talk with them about the way they see the privileges of the final Infant year: what they would like to be allowed to do. *(Distributing registers, ringing bells, taking messages, etc.)* Explain that with privileges comes responsibility in doing the coveted jobs properly and efficiently.

Older Infants will look to the time when they will move up and already they may be envying older brothers and sisters who come home to talk about their experiences and activities at a higher level in school. Could your children visit an older class? Or could you arrange that for this particular week the children in your class take over one or two of the duties normally assigned to older children? They would then see for themselves the responsibilities that are laid upon the shoulders of the others.

Let the children draw or write about someone they would most like to be. Talk with them about the reasons for their choice; what they most envy in that person, and then about that person's special responsibilities.

The Assembly

Hymns and songs

When we are happy, full of fun	NCS 29
At half past three we go home to tea	NCS 43 SSL 38
Babies are tiny	NCS 98
Jesus' hands were kind hands	SSL 33

Poem

Discontent

Why can't I go to bed at nine,
just like my brother Jim?
Oh how I wish that I could stay
awake as long as him!

Why can't my Mummy hold me like
the baby in her arms?
Or coo at me, and pat my back,
and play games on my palms?

Sometimes I try to look as old
as Jim, who's nearly ten;
But Daddy looks at me and says
I can wash dishes then!

And yesterday I made a fuss,
and cried like baby did;
'Now don't be silly,' Mummy said,
and so I went and hid.

They don't know how I feel at all,
when Jim gets all the praise
and baby gets the cuddles—I'm
just told to mend my ways!

I don't like Jim; the baby's mean
to steal my Mummy's time;
I wish my parents just had me,
and all the toys were mine!

I s'pose I'll grow to love them all,
we'll be good friends one day;
I wish that time would come right now!
Meanwhile, I'll go and play!

Prayer

Dear Father God,
 to you I pray:
please take my fears
and hate away.

Dear Father God,
 please help me be
the one to love
those dear to me.

Dear Father God,
 help me to grow,
to let my love
and caring show.

Dear Father God,
 I'll hold your hand,
and in your love
I'll understand.

Stories

Bible stories: Joseph and his jealous brothers—Genesis 37.11-28
               Andrew wants the best for his brother—John 1.35-42
Oliver goes shopping (told in full)

Oliver goes shopping

'Now keep hold of Ian's hand,' Mother warned as the two boys went down the front path. 'Come straight back, and don't forget to call at the chemist's, Ian. I've run right out of shampoo for the baby.'

Oliver held Ian's hand tightly. It was not often the two boys were allowed out together on a special mission, and Oliver did not want to stop it happening again. Ian had often been to the shops by himself. He was big and quite old: he was soon going into the fourth year at Primary School, while Oliver had only been going to school for two terms. He remembered feeling very strange indeed when he went to school for the first time, as if he was being pulled in two directions at once, like a piece of elastic. He wanted to start school, to learn to read and write like Ian did, to play big boys' games like Ian did, and to come home with drawings and letters and special pieces of writing like Ian did. But he did not want to leave Mummy, and he felt as if she were pushing him out. She was always saying things like, 'Thank goodness you'll be at school soon, Oliver' and, 'Do go and play with something, you can see I'm busy now'. She was only busy because she'd brought home a baby to look after—a girl! And that baby seemed to take up all of Mummy's time. When she was hungry, Mummy rushed to her with a bottle of milk; when she screamed, Mummy hurried to pick her up and cuddle her; even when she was fast asleep Mummy was doing all sorts of things for her, like

99

washing her clothes, or preparing her next feed.

'Have you still got the money?' Oliver asked Ian, as they walked towards the zebra crossing.

'Of course I have,' said Ian, and opened his hand to show his little brother. There were three coins: one small gold coloured one, which was £1, and two bigger silver ones, which were 50p pieces.

'Let me hold one of them,' said Oliver.

'No,' said Ian, 'you'll lose it.'

Oliver sighed. When would *he* be old enough to hold the money and go shopping all by himself?

They stood on the pavement by the zebra crossing. 'We can go across!' said Oliver, jumping from the kerb to the gutter and back again.

'Get back and keep still,' said Ian crossly. 'We've got to wait until the road is quite clear, or until all the traffic stops for us.'

Oliver sighed again. He did not like waiting. He thought they could easily have got across between the cars, but Ian held him back until it was quite safe.

'We'll get the loaf of bread first,' said Ian, looking at Mummy's shopping list. 'Then we'll go and buy the oranges and bananas at the greengrocer's. You can carry the oranges.'

While Ian asked for the bread at the baker's, Oliver hopped from one foot to the other looking at the iced buns and chocolate éclairs. 'Buy one of those, Ian,' he said. 'We can eat it before we get home. Mummy won't know!'

'Yes, she will,' said Ian. 'We won't have the right change.'

Oliver had not thought of that. Ian was clever. But it must be a nuisance to have to think of how much change Mummy would expect to have.

At the greengrocer's shop Ian asked for five oranges and four bananas. How clever of him to remember just how many Mummy had wanted; but how good his memory had to be. Oliver could never remember anything. He clutched at the bag of oranges.

'It's too heavy,' he announced, and left it on the counter for Ian to pick up. The lady gave Ian a carrier-bag, which Oliver thought he might be able to manage better than the brown paper one which held the oranges. He grabbed the carrier-bag out of Ian's hand, but it was so heavy he dropped it on the floor.

'Leave it alone,' Ian said to Oliver. 'I'll carry it.'

Ian tried hard to keep hold of Oliver's hand as they left the shop, but it was difficult with a loaf of bread under his arm, the loose change in one hand, and a carrier-bag in the other hand. He put the bread into the carrier-bag. It was even heavier now, and he had to hold it high to stop it dragging along the ground beside him.

In the chemist's shop Ian asked for the baby's shampoo.

'I'm sorry, dear, we're right out of that kind,' said the assistant. 'The others are just as good, though. Take one of them.'

'Let's go home,' said Oliver, who was getting restless.

'No, I must think,' said Ian. 'Mum hasn't got any shampoo for the baby, so I'd better get something, but which one would she like?'

Oliver was surprised. Shopping was not as easy as he thought. You had to ask for the right things, you had to look after the change, you had to carry heavy loads, and now you had to decide things.

'I'll take this one,' said Ian, and counted out the money carefully as the lady assistant put the bottle of shampoo into a paper bag. Now he had exactly 17p to take back home: a 10p piece, a 5p piece, and two 1p pieces. 'You can carry the shampoo,' he said to Oliver. 'It's in a plastic bottle, so you can't break it.' How sensible of Ian to think of that, Oliver thought.

Oliver wanted to run all the way home once they had crossed the zebra crossing again, and Ian had to make a grab at him. The coins shot out of his hand and rolled all over the path. The two boys picked them up.

At last they were home again. Oliver put the paper bag with the shampoo in it into Mother's hand, then rushed in to turn on the TV set so that he could watch *Playschool*. He heard Mother and Ian talking in the hall. Ian was explaining about the shampoo.

'How much change did you have?' asked Mother.

'Seventeen pence,' said Ian, and opened up his hand.

'You've only seven pence there,' said Mother. 'Where's the rest of it?'

'I dropped it all—but I thought I picked it up,' said Ian.

'That was a bit careless,' said Mother. 'Where did you drop it?'

'Just up the road,' Ian told her.

'Then I think you'd better go straight back and try to find it,' said Mother, and Ian walked wearily out of the front door again.

Now it was Oliver's turn to think hard. Being old and big like Ian was not all fun. He had had to work really hard at shopping: he had had to look after Oliver, make decisions, make sure he bought all the things he was sent out for, and be grown up about the money. Oliver sat back and watched the TV. He felt lucky, and lazy. One day he would do all the things Ian did, but until then he would enjoy himself being not quite old enough.

And the baby was yelling again. She must be too hot, or too cold, or too wet, or starving hungry. It could not be much fun being her, either!

101

Pictures to look at

Project outline

Without trying to impose personal artistic preferences, this project aims at getting the children to look at pictures around them, so that they begin to appreciate artistic things, and cease to treat them as part of a room's furnishings.

Start by looking round the school for framed pictures; the extent of this exploratory survey will depend, of course, on the number of pictures on show. Take the children to look at as many as possible, and talk about the subject-matter in each. Artistic merit and competence need not be issues under discussion, but it is worthwhile taking note of the reactions of the boys and girls. Do they, generally, prefer pictures that tell a story, or landscapes, flowers, portraits or abstracts? How much do they seem influenced in their preferences by colours, medium, shape or size? Do they seem to know the difference between a photo and a painting or a reproduction?

Back in the class-room, talk about the pictures. List them and make a chart of their popularity. Ask the children to draw as much of their favourite picture as they can remember.

In another session, ask about pictures in their homes. Have they really noticed the pictures that hang on the walls, and can they recall the subject-matter of any of them? If their recall is poor, suggest they go round the rooms at home that evening and really look at the pictures, so that they can be discussed next day. This further talk together may lead to you being able to identify any well-known reproductions, of which you should make a note. Ask about photographs too; why these are precious to families, and why they are displayed.

It will be helpful, at this stage, if you can find out anything about the artist of one of the pictures displayed in your school, or the artist of a picture you can take into the class-room from home. There are plenty of library books about painters of well-known pictures, which will provide information and further illustrations.

Very young children are under the impression that every adult can draw well. Some of the least artistic teachers are flattered to find their blackboard drawings applauded with enthusiasm! But it is a natural step from a discussion about pictures to talking about artists in general, and about the gift they possess which they are willing (and, in some cases, impelled) to share with society.

Other forms of artistic talent can be mentioned, such as a talent for music, for dancing, for acting, and for writing. Who gives these talents, and why should they be used for mankind, rather than used in secret, unseen and unshared?

Although in modern versions of the Bible the parable of the talents, told by Jesus, is given the context of money, it is an apt one when talking about our own, or other people's, talents as gifts. (Matthew 25.14-29; a talent was a silver coin.) Remember that the talents of drawing and painting, as opposed to some of the other arts, are largely dormant until after puberty, so try not to pick out children who are particularly good, or bad, at art at this early age.

Speak about how the truly gifted artist can, in a painting, make very ordinary things extraordinarily beautiful. This is part of their gift, involving seeing as well as wielding a brush, and it is a difficult concept to get across to young children. To appreciate this yourself, look at a photograph of a chair, and then compare it with Van Gogh's *The Yellow Chair* (in the National Gallery).

At the end of this short preparation time before the Assembly, you will have achieved something if you have been able to make the children take an interest in works of art—good or bad—around them, and made them aware that the gifts of an artist come from God. Collect together some pictures to display at the Assembly; postcards and books will also be useful.

The story of Henri Rousseau (1844-1910) is told briefly for the actual Assembly. Many schools have reproductions of his pictures, which are painted in the Primitive style.

The Assembly

Hymns and songs

Look up! Look up!	NCS 1
Skipping down the pavement wide	NCS 36
Give to us eyes	SSL 18
I danced in the morning	SSL 29

Music
   Pictures at an Exhibition, Mussorgsky

Poem

Pictures

Pictures which hang upon the wall
can be a pleasure to us all!
  A painting of this land of ours,
  with all its hills and trees and flowers;
and portraits of the folk we know,
or people who lived long ago;
   or animals, or fish or birds—
   artists have no need of words.
Paintings from years gone by can come,
through prints, into our school or home.
  We should be happy we can see
  the gifts they shared with all, and be
  part of their world—see as they saw—
  their work lives on, for evermore!

Prayer

  Thank you, Lord God, for men and women who have given us beautiful things to look at. Help us to use our eyes and hands so that we may make lovely things ourselves.

Stories

  Bible stories: Moses selects men with God's gifts to make the Tent of the
              Lord's Presence beautiful—Exodus 31.1-11 (use a modern
              version)
             The parable of the talents—Matthew 25.14-29
  Henri's happiness (told in full)

Henri's happiness

Henri Rousseau never had any money. He had got a job, but it was paid so badly that he often felt very hungry. He worked by a bridge, collecting money from farmers with carts, women with large barrows going to market, and important officials riding into town with their smart horses and carriages. Sometimes, particularly when the weather was bad, no one went over the little bridge, and Henri would have no work to do. But he did not mind, because he had something else he liked doing very much, and when he was not busy he could do this instead. Everyone in the little French town liked Henri : he always had a cheery word and a smile, however hungry he was, or however cold.

When he was a little boy, Henri had always liked drawing, but he had never had any lessons to show him exactly how to do it, or a teacher to show him how to use the paint. When he grew up, he bought himself some paints, a few brushes, and set about sawing up sheets of old wood on which to paint pictures. Every day he painted, and soon his little house was filled with pictures. They were hung all over the walls and on the backs of the doors, and were stacked in every corner. Nobody ever bought one from him, because nobody thought they were very good; they even laughed at them.

'My little boy can paint better than that!' people used to say.

So Henri stayed a poor man. His clothes had many patches and his shoes were worn right through.

'We can't understand how he keeps so happy,' his neighbours said. 'He's always smiling, as if something inside was lit up with the secret of life!'

One day Henri actually managed to sell a painting for a small sum, and you should have seen him jump up and down for joy! He wanted to share his fortune straight away, and invited all his friends and neighbours to a party. Everybody crowded into his little house, and they sang and danced until it was nearly morning. Henri himself played the violin for them to dance to, and the grocer from the shop up the road recited poetry.

When Henri was getting old, he became interested in painting pictures showing jungles. He never had enough money to visit tropical forests to see wild animals living there, so he had to go to the zoo in Paris and draw the animals in cages. He also visited the big greenhouses where rich and lovely tropical plants grew, and got to know their colours, shapes and patterns, so that he could go home and make huge pictures of what he imagined jungles to be like. He painted tigers stepping through long grass under waving jungle trees and hanging plants, and gorillas and buffaloes hidden by grass and ferns. His little room began to look green and jungly itself as more and more pictures stood agianst the walls. His friends said that Henri seemed even more filled with love and joy at the richness of the world he painted but had never seen.

If Henri Rousseau were alive today he would be happier still to see prints of his pictures everywhere, in schools and houses, in important places as well as ordinary homes. Some of them have been made into birthday cards, too. He wanted lots of people to see them; he would have been glad to share his gift of painting with them all.

(From facts in Readers Digest *Great Painters and Great Paintings* 1965)

Helping those in need

Project outline

This project is designed to give the children some awareness of the work done by charities to help underprivileged people in our own country and abroad. That we need charities is unfortunate; that they exist tells us something about the concern felt by the majority of people for the deprived, homeless, ill-treated, and starving people of the world.

It is necessary first to show the children how some people are forced to live: as refugees, in poverty, in places where rain and food are very scarce, in fear, and in loneliness. Through the media, scenes of such deprivation and humiliation are familiar to most of us, and our children, yet it is still possible for individuals to be unmoved and unconcerned, and so self-interested that the needs of other people do not touch them. Let the children look at pictures of those in great need. It is likely that some will be upset, so do not dwell on the horrific scenes for too long. Remember that a normally privileged child who is touched or moved by knowing how others live is more likely to grow into a caring adult than those who can think only of themselves and their own needs.

From the pictures of people who need help, pass on to the people who give help, the charities and organisations which ask for our money, time, prayers, and other forms of aid. There is a wealth of these charities to choose from; select about three, and find out more of what they are doing. Send for literature, ask for a visit from one of their representatives, and plan an activity that could result in some money being sent to that charity. If the children can also write letters, poems, or produce pictures to send to the charity, it will deepen their interest, especially if an acknowledgement or reply comes to the class directly from the charity concerned.

Papier-mâché money boxes might be made, together with appeal notices and posters. Involve the whole class in planning how to pass on to the Assembly the information gained, and the schemes planned for future help for the chosen charities.

The Assembly

Poem
Zuby and I
Dad has a motor, and I have a bike,
  and even the baby will soon ride a trike,
Mum has a mixer, and washing machine,
  and we all have a telly, with a great big screen.

We have a garden to sit in at home,
  a place where my friends can play when they come;
we go on holiday once every year,
  and we all get excited when we know it's near.

Zuby has nothing, not even a home;
  she camps in the open, and then has to roam;
she begs for her food, and searches the ground
  for places where water can sometimes be found.

She dresses in rags, her mother does too—
  it doesn't seem likely they'll have something new.
The baby is crying, he's got a bad pain,
  and Zuby joins in—she's hungry again.

Just think what it's like to be Zuby out there,
  with not enough water to wash clothes or hair;
to wander all day in the heat of the sun,
  and never to laugh, because laughing's no fun.

I wish I could help you, and people like you,
  dear Zuby, dear baby, and your mother too.
I'll give what I can, and I just want to say
  I will think of you often as I pray each day.

(This poem will have more impact if contrasting pictures of a home in this country and conditions of deprived people are held up. Zuby is an East African name.)

Lord, we know that children suffer, and we ask that you will show us ways in which we can help them. We thank you that each day people are working to try to help the needy; give them strength to do their work well. Take the gifts, however small, that we offer.

Stories
Bible story: Jesus helps a deaf and dumb man—Mark 7.31-37
Everyone can help (told in full)

Everyone can help

Ricky lived in the same northern town as Old Jim, and he got to know him quite well. Everyone who knew Old Jim said that he was a wonderful old man. Quite often Ricky and his friends would go out to the hill above the town where they knew he would be, and chat to him as he walked. He never strolled, as old men often do, but strode out so fast that the boys had a job to keep up with him.

One day they found him up there, his white hair looking like goose feathers ruffled by the wind and rain, and he was panting, as if he had been running hard.

'Have you been a long way?' asked Ricky.

'About two miles,' said Old Jim, getting his breath back, 'but I haven't left this spot!'

Ricky couldn't think how Old Jim had walked, or run, two miles without moving, so he laughed.

'It's no laughing matter, lad,' said Jim. 'I've been doing a bit of jogging on the spot. Gets the feet and legs going, you know.'

'What for?' asked Ricky. Old Jim must be at least seventy-five.

'For walking, boy, walking,' said Old Jim, and began striding away down the hill back to the town.

Ricky and his friends watched him go. The town below looked grey; huge chimneys poked up at the sky, and factories stood side by side along the streets. Ricky did not want to go back down. The little houses were jumbled together, as if someone had emptied them out of a sack, but he could just make out the roof of his own house, and the tiny patch of garden where his mother had planted her seeds. So many of the houses had no gardens at all; some had backyards that were full of junk, and others looked out over massive rubbish tips, or were face to face with factory windows. Lots of Ricky's school friends lived down there, in poky little rooms, and had nowhere to play except the streets. Mother said she knew several families who had never been to the seaside for a holiday, and where the children never had new clothes, only ones passed on to them by other people.

Old Jim had quite disappeared, and rain had started to fall, so Ricky and his friends ran back over the grass and stones until they reached the corner of their road.

'See you at school tomorrow,' shouted Ricky as he ran along the pavement to his house. 'Old Jim has been jogging,' he told his mother at tea-time.

'Grand old man,' said his father. 'Lots of people round here call him "Ironlegs". He's jolly strong, considering his age.'

Ironlegs; Ricky thought about it for a moment. Legs made of iron: no wonder he could walk for miles!

'Are his legs really iron?' he asked, wondering how Old Jim could bend them to sit down comfortably. And they must be awfully heavy!

'No!' said Dad with a laugh. 'That's just his nickname. But they do seem as strong as iron, when you think of all the walking he does. Out in all kinds of weather, too.'

'Have you heard what he's planning to do next?' Mother asked. 'Mrs Barnes was telling me about it in the supermarket. He's going to walk as many times round Aintree race-track as he can, to raise money for the children.'

'What children?' asked Ricky. Perhaps he'd get some!

'For those who need holidays, or who are treated badly—knocked about,' said Mother. 'Some need a real treat, too: new toys, or clothes, or a visit to Chester Zoo.'

'Does Old Jim collect the money as he goes round the race-track?' asked Ricky.

'No. People promise him ten pence or fifteen pence for every mile he walks round it,' said Mother. 'I said I'd give something. We ought to help those children somehow.'

Ricky thought he'd like to help them too. 'Can I give twopence out of my pocket-money for every mile Old Jim walks round?' he asked. His mother said it was a lovely idea.

Lots of people were beside the race-track at Aintree to watch Old Jim — Ironlegs. He wore a special track-suit.

'Are your feet and legs going all right?' Ricky managed to ask him.

'Yes, lad, they'll be fine,' said Old Jim, and the people cheered as he started walking. The racecourse was very big. You could not see all round it from one place, so Old Jim was soon out of sight. People were unpacking picnics and sitting on the grass, waiting for him to come round again.

Ricky and his parents stayed there for a long time, waving and cheering each time Ironlegs appeared. He was still going strong. Mother said that Ricky could go there again with Dad after tea, to see if Old Jim was still walking.

The sun was going down when they returned to the racecourse, but Old Jim was still walking round!

'He's been going for nine hours,' a man watching told them. 'Looks quite fresh, too! Seems to be going quite steady still.'

They waited until Old Jim came past again. 'You're great, Old Jim!' shouted Ricky at the top of his voice, and everyone began to clap.

Next morning the announcer on local radio said that Old Jim Ratcliffe, 'Ironlegs', had kept on walking for twelve hours. He had raised a terrific amount of money for charity, too, for the children who really needed it.

Dad showed Ricky a map. 'Old Jim walked forty-five miles,' he said. 'Look, that's about as far as from Wigan to Liverpool—and back!'

Ricky could hardly believe it; it always seemed such a long way to Liverpool, and that was in the car!

Next time Ricky met Old Jim on the hill above the town, he gave him ninety pence out of his money-box. 'This is for you to help the poor children,' he explained.

'They'll be right pleased,' said Old Jim, grinning. 'I'll put it with all the rest. Thanks for helping, lad.'

'I think I'll earn some money for the children myself,' Ricky told his parents later on. His mother and father seemed really glad, and promised to think of a way he could help by raising money. His father picked up the newspaper, and read a little bit out to Ricky. 'Young people, as well as the very old,' he read, 'are collecting money for the charity that helps children, and hundreds of boys and girls will be able to have happier lives because of the help they are being given.'

Ricky smiled. 'I'm one of the very young,' he said, 'and Jim is one of the very old. The paper didn't say anything about the in-betweens, like you, Mum and Dad, did it? But we're all going to help, aren't we?'

(Facts from NSPCC *Centenary Express*, July 1984)

Dealing with aggression

Project outline

Even young children become spectators of violence and aggression. Television screens show brutality, either fictional or actual, in plays, documentaries and news bulletins; few children are completely protected from it. Sadly, many children also see aggression in their own homes, often as a prelude to the separation and divorce of parents. Animals are equipped with claws and teeth for fighting, but aggression in humans results in the use of weapons, which become ever more deadly and destructive.

But aggression can have a constructive side: man uses it to strive to master his environment, as part of his struggle for existence. Aggression leads to winning, in competitive sports, in the academic and business world, and often in artistic achievement. Driving oneself on to achievement can be good, but not at the expense of other people. Aggression, unchannelled, can be dangerous; but self-assertiveness, coupled with energy and determinaton, can be constructive, and has produced some of the world's finest men and women.

Much childish aggression stems from the home environment. If there are signs of it in the children in your care, then look for hints of parental rejection or harsh punishment.

The way teachers, and authorities in general, deal with such behaviour is a constant source of speculation. Some say that harsh discipline is the only answer; others advocate, as a Christian viewpoint, that aggression should be treated with understanding. We often see that harsh punishment only teaches how to punish, and scolding teaches how to scold. Diversion, occupation elsewhere, or systematic channelling of anger, seem to be immediate ways of dealing with aggressive behaviour; understanding it, and the person using it, is a long-term, difficult undertaking.

The decision to conduct an Assembly which deals with aggression will probably be made after it has been encountered in the class-room or in the playground. Probably the best time to begin is immediately you are called upon to deal with angry or violent behaviour between pupils in the school.

Gather all the children in the class together to talk about what has happened. Try not to take sides, or encourage the onlookers to do so. Ask questions such as,

111

'What would you have done if that had happened to you?' 'How would you have felt?' The aggressive child, or children, may then realise that angry feelings and reactions are not uncommon, or bad in themselves, but that it is what they can lead to that is destructive and harmful. The other children in the class will also begin to think about the problems that people with such violent reactions to anger have—which is the beginning of understanding.

Discuss what might have happened instead of the confrontation: there could have been a retreat from the situation; anger could have been directed against an inanimate object (and not against the other child), or there could even have been a more positive decision to involve the other child in some different activity. This last is by far the most difficult for an aggressive child, but should be shown as an alternative.

Let the children draw or write about situations in which they have felt anger. Discuss these together later, to see if alternative behaviour could be used in any of them. To be able to look ahead, seeing a way out, might help some of the children, although most young children find curbing immediate aggression almost impossible, as their control at the time is very limited.

Next, talk with them about times when anger is necessary, eg, when seeing someone beat a puppy, and how, in this case, justified anger could be a means of ending misery and cruelty.

Show, too, how a degree of aggression is often necessary to winning, not by pushing, bullying or anger, but by fighting with oneself to push oneself to the limit. Demonstrate this in a practical way by having races or competitions on the field or in the playground. It will probably be best to divide the class for these races, putting all the good runners and athletes in one race, and the less energetic in another, so that competition is for their own endeavour, however naturally good or bad at sport they may be.

Try an activity also where the children can hit, bang, or beat objects. This will probably be a noisy session, so keep it short and out of earshot! As in the sporting activities, get the children to use up as much energy as possible, then lead them straight into a quiet story or poetry session.

The Assembly

Hymns and songs

Let's beat a song of praise	NCS 71
Peter works with one hammer	NCS 99
Lord, I love to stamp and shout	SSL 5
When a knight won his spurs	SSL 34

Poem

Animals all different

Fighting as a lion,
  hissing as a snake,
angry like a tiger,
  snarl and growl and shake!

Pretty as a parrot,
  silent as a bat,
singing like a blackbird,
  purring like a cat!

Running like a cheetah,
  crawling as a snail,
jumping like a puppy
  chasing for his tail!

Animals all different
  just like you and me;
gentle or ferocious,
  which one will you be?

Music

The Miraculous Mandarin, Bartok
English Idylls, Butterworth
On Hearing the First Cuckoo in Spring, Delius
(The dance by Bartok contains some very aggressive passages which could be
used at the beginning of the Assembly or as background to the activity in the
Assembly. This is then contrasted with the other music.)

Prayer

Lord, let me use my strong hands
in the kindest way;
  let them be more gentle
  than they are today.

I can think of hitting out,
shouting loudly, too.
  now I'm really sorry—
  it was hurting you.

Dear Jesus, find some good work
for my hands today:
  keep them free from fighting;
  check the words I say.

Lord, let me use my strong hands
for what's good and true,
  for when they are gentle,
  I am more like you.

Awful and Evil

Orville and Evan Clarke were twins, boys not much older than the youngest children here. They were born in a town in the South of England, but their mother and father had been born in Jamaica, and had come to Britain to work. Father Clarke was big and black, with shining white teeth and a huge smile. Mother Clarke was large and round, and could hug both the boys with one big strong arm. It was not surprising that the boys were big for their age, and as strongly built as bullocks.

Because there were always the two of them, Orville and Evan were never lonely when they started school, and they laughed at the children who cried, or who could not do up their coat buttons, or who were not strong enough to run around the playground twice before school started.

It was not long before they began to get into mischief. Together, they thought up the most terrible tricks, and were always getting into trouble. Miss Gurney, the head teacher, decided to talk to them.

'Well, you two,' she said sternly, 'I've been hearing about you a lot lately. What did you do this morning that made Miss Sherwood send you in from the playground?'

Orville looked straight at Miss Gurney. 'It wasn't me,' he said. 'It was Evan.' The twins were so alike that nobody could tell them apart.

Miss Gurney looked at Evan. He grinned—his father's huge smile. 'I wasn't doing anything!' he said cheerfully.

Miss Gurney decided to watch the twins from her window when they went out to play that afternoon. Miss Sherwood's class went out a minute or two before everybody else. Evan and Orville rushed out of the cloakroom like tanks. A little girl was knocked over, and a boy had to step aside to avoid being ploughed into, but the twins did not seem even to notice! The boy ran after them, and when he caught them up, he stood in front of them. For one minute Miss Gurney thought he was going to run away, but he stood still. Evan pushed him, but he still did not move. Then Orville took the boy's arm and twisted it. It hurt a lot.

'You bully-boys!' the boy shouted. Evan and Orville laughed, and ran off, shouting and yelling, their legs kicking children out of the way as they went. They rushed round the playground, tormenting younger children, and picking fights with boys in the top class. One of these boys shouted at Orville, and Evan, hearing him, became really angry. He picked up a stone and hurled it, hitting the boy on his arm. Miss Sherwood, on playground duty, hurried over. There was a real fight going on, hands hitting, feet kicking, and the twins' eyes blazed with fury. Miss Sherwood tried to move Evan to one side; it was like trying to move a rock at the seaside! She grabbed Orville's coat, but Orville kicked and screamed. Miss Gurney, watching from her window, decided it was time she went outside to help Miss Sherwood. The twins saw her coming.

'IN!' ordered Miss Gurney, and she marched them back into school. She could quite understand why the teachers had nicknamed the twins 'Awful and Evil'! 'Sit there and don't move!' Miss Gurney said. She would let them calm down a bit while she was deciding what to do with them. She went into her office. Perhaps she could teach them a lesson by slapping them hard! But, she thought, they already knew how to hit hard—it would not really teach them anything! Perhaps she should shout at them, but they had been shouting themselves, and she would be behaving in exactly the same way if she shouted too, and that would not help.

Suddenly she had an idea. 'Come in here, Evan and Orville,' she called. The twins stood on the mat by her table, their eyes still bright with anger, and their fists clenched behind their backs. 'I've got a job for you two,' said Miss Gurney.

The twins could not think what had happened. They had been expecting a smack, or a few sharp words, but not a job!

Miss Gurney took them to the window. 'You see that low wall?' she asked. It had once been a high wall, and workmen had pulled most of it down so that now it was only three bricks high, and not dangerous. But it was in the way. 'Next playtime,' went on Miss Gurney, 'I want you to start knocking the rest of it down for me. You are both big and strong, two of my best lads when it comes to strength! Use that strength sensibly! Ask the caretaker for two mallets, and get it all knocked down. I'll see that whoever's on playground duty keeps the other children out of the way; we don't want any accidents, do we?'

Orville and Evan agreed; they didn't really want to hurt anyone. They knew they were strong—now they could actually use their strength to help someone.

The twins did not have to give up their playtimes altogether, but from then on every time they felt angry or cross, whenever they felt they wanted to hit or kick someone, they ran to the little wall and knocked away a few bricks.

Evan and Orville are almost grown up now. They are still big and very strong; Orville is hoping to be a professional footballer, and Evan is training to be a builder. They do still get angry sometimes, as most people do, but now they know what to do about it.

115

Grey

Project outline

The very word *grey* conjures up ideas of depression, sadness and drabness. Grey skies, grey hairs, grey areas, all these are things that probably we would rather not think about, as they have connotations with stormy weather, old age, and indeterminate regions. Grey is almost a nothing in itself. It is an intermediate shade between black and white, a colour made from two no-colour, or achromatic, pigments. Grey is all round us: streets and pavements and playgrounds are, for the most part, grey; many roof tiles are grey, ash is grey; newspapers are grey, made up as they are of black characters on white newsprint, alongside the photographs that appear in them. Some people view television in black and white (and therefore grey). Twilight and dawn are times when all other colours are swallowed up in the greyness, times when it is neither dark nor light.

But there are degrees of grey, from almost black to almost white; from the blue-grey of slate to the silver-grey of a cod's scales; from the brown-grey bark of a walnut tree to the pink-grey velvet of a mouse's ear. Grey, as a pigment, is often overlooked, neglected, or shunned. In this project we shall try to find beauty in it, together with anticipation and hope.

From the several suggestions given here pick those areas which will suit your children best, and spark off their interest and enthusiasm.

Elephants Look at pictures of elephants in the wild or in zoos: wallowing in the mud, or herding to protect their young. Discover how they help man, how they are hunted by him, and how much they need his protection. Note the differences between the African elephant and the Indian; look closely at their grey wrinkled hide, and at their eyes and tusks. Make lists of words that best describe them, such as enormous, strong, etc. Make a large class-room picture of an elephant in paint or collage, and let the children write about what they have learnt. Some may be able to write poems or stories about imaginary elephants. Include a variety of stimulating stories yourself, such as those from the *Just So Stories* by Kipling, *Babar the Elephant* and so on. If you plan to include the elephant discoveries in the Assembly, write the words GREY IS STRENGTH for display there.

Clouds Talk briefly and simply about clouds, vapour, and why we sometimes say 'Those clouds look as if they will bring rain'. How can we recognise rain and storm clouds? What colour are they? What would it be like if it never rained? This could be an opportunity to talk about drought and famine experienced by people who rely on rain. Make a frieze of a landscape or town silhouetted below a blue sky, with cotton wool (white and shaded grey) stuck on for clouds. Discuss how we feel when we see the sun coming out again after rain. How many children have noticed the sun and sky reflected in grey puddles? When asked to draw rain puddles, most children will colour them grey, but examine some together and get the children to see what colours they *really* have. Some children could paint what they saw in them. Others might depict the rain itself, falling on ground which is sprouting seedlings. These pieces of work could all be displayed at the Assembly under the words GREY CAN GIVE FOOD AND HEALTH.

Cygnets Study pictures of a swan's nest, built of sticks, leaves and soft down, built on ground close to water. The eggs are large and usually pale grey-green. The cygnets which hatch are grey, awkward and unlovely, especially while they are on dry land. Tell the story of the ugly duckling, of how the uninteresting grey chick grows to be as white and graceful as his parents. A group of children might dramatise the story for the Assembly, and show a notice which says, GREY CAN BECOME BEAUTIFUL.

Pebbles If it is possible to visit a seashore, look at the rocks and pebbles there. Notice how they change colour when covered in water. They may still retain their greyness, but the colour looks much richer under water. You may also, or instead, be able to obtain some natural gems, the grey rock cut to reveal hidden colours and designs. Ask a local jeweller to come and tell the children how rocks and pebbles can be 'tumbled' to make them shine and show their beauty. He might be able to produce some examples, or pictures, of silver and gold in their natural state—uninteresting to all but an expert's eye. Make a collection of stones and pebbles; a coat of varnish will give the same effect as water on them. Show items at the Assembly with the words, GREY HIDES BEAUTIFUL COLOURS.

Oil Although not all oil is grey, it can appear so when spilled on a grey road or the forecourt of a garage. It is this spilled oil which can hold such fascination for children and adults alike. Do some experiments with oil and water. Watch the oil float, as it does in puddles, and see it spread with the rainbow colours. Count and name the colours found. Talk about this to the rest of the school at Assembly, and hold up a sign saying, GREY IS SOMETIMES FULL OF COLOUR.

Old age   It would be suitable here to invite an old person to visit your class, a man or woman who has grey (not white) hair, to talk to the children, quite informally, about an exciting or interesting thing that has happened to them, or an event from the past that they witnessed, or about their schooldays. The children will probably be fascinated by the old person's memories, for to young children old people do not have a past: they feel that they can never have been young. Later, talk about what the children heard and suggest that, when they themselves are old and grey, they may be able to visit a school to talk about their own adventures and experiences. The children will probably be able to talk about the wisdom and understanding that older people have acquired, and how their experiences really can help those growing up today. Some children could tell the Assembly about the visit of the old person. Their notice could bear the quotation GREY HAIR IS A GLORIOUS CROWN (Proverbs 16.31, GNB).

During the project, collect a display of things that are grey—pictures of elephants, mice, clouds, etc; black and white photographs and newspapers; grey stones, feathers, material, shells, ash, etc. The items will show many variations of colour within the grey scale.

The Assembly

Hymns and songs

What do we see when we go to the town?	NCS 35
Skipping down the pavement wide	NCS 36
Come let us remember the joys of the town (v.2)	SSL 7
The ink is black, the page is white	SSL 39

Poem

Grey skies

The skies today
are grey;
and grey the town,
pavements and roads,
and workmen's loads
are dark grey-brown.

But look again
in rain:
silver the grey,
shining and bright,
washed overnight,
grey can be gay.

Music

  Bolero, Ravel
  (This piece has a repetitive theme without any contrasts [grey] except for the
  different instruments used and the increasing crescendo: like the colour grey,
  when this piece is explored it becomes interesting to listen to)

Prayer

  We have seen, Lord God, that grey can be a lovely colour when we look at it
  properly. Help us to look for the best everywhere we go, so that we can see
  beauty where other people see only ugliness. You have given us a lovely
  world, O Lord.

Stories

  Bible story: The story of Noah, adapted to suit the age group, with emphasis
              on the grey dove and the beautiful rainbow—Genesis 7—9
  From grey to gold (told in full)

From grey to gold

In the garden of number 23 London Road there was a mulberry tree. Every year
in the spring Mrs Cooper said to Mr Cooper that the old tree was dead.

'Wait a bit,' said Mr Cooper wisely, every year. 'It's always later than the
other trees. It's all right.' And every year Mr Cooper was right. Long after the
willow tree was in leaf, and just as the pink blossom was bursting on the apple
trees, the old mulberry unfolded its leaves. It had been there as long as Mr Cooper
had, and he had lived in the house as a child.

'When I was seven,' he told Mrs Cooper, often, 'I kept silkworms, and we fed
them on mulberry leaves.'

Mrs Cooper was not interested in silkworms, but one day when their
grandchildren, Sandra and Tom, came to call on them, she had a surprise.

'Look what I've bought for you,' Mr Cooper said to them. 'Some silkworm
eggs. Now you can watch them hatch, and you can call in every day after school
to feed them mulberry leaves. We'll put them in the garden shed.'

'How shall we carry them out there?' asked Tom, looking at the tiny grey eggs
on the white paper. 'If they fall off we won't be able to see them on the ground, or
pick them up.'

Mr Cooper lifted the paper and turned it upside-down. The eggs stayed where
they were.

'They're stuck on!' said Sandra. 'Doesn't that hurt them?'

'Oh no,' said Grandfather. 'When the mother moth lays them they are sticky
and white and soft. As they dry hard they turn grey, and are stuck to whatever she

lays them on.'

They carried the paper with the eggs on it out to the shed in a shallow box. 'They'll hatch in a day or two,' said Grandfather. Sure enough, when Sandra and Tom went back to look at them five days later they could see very small black things moving over the paper, like creeping pencil marks.

'They're awfully small!' said Tom. 'And not very interesting.'

'Go and pick some mulberry leaves,' said Mr Cooper, 'and lay them on the paper beside the silkworms. Those little creatures know what to do.'

After they had drunk their orange juice and eaten their biscuits, the children went to have another look at the silkworms. 'They've gone!' said Sandra, looking all round and underneath the flat box.

'No, no,' laughed Grandfather. 'Lift up that leaf, very gently, and you'll see them.' Sure enough, all the worms were on the leaf. 'They've already begun to eat,' he went on, 'and look, all the egg cases are white again. The tiny silkworms inside them made them look grey.'

It was a week before Sandra and Tom could visit their grandparents again. Grandfather had kept the tiny silkworms supplied with fresh mulberry leaves every day. 'Just look at them now,' he said. 'You'll hardly recognise them.'

When Sandra and Tom looked in the box the little black marks had grown into tiny grey caterpillars, each about a centimetre long. They gasped, 'They're not worms at all!' Tom said, rather sadly. 'They're caterpillars—plain old grey caterpillars!' and he stalked out.

But Sandra looked at them carefully. They certainly were caterpillars, with six tiny feet and legs at the front of their bodies, and several pairs of strong stumps at the other end. She watched them moving, creeping slowly about among the leaves. They were eating hungrily, hardly stopping.

Sandra came in every day, but Tom was often too busy with his friends. 'You can feed those boring grey caterpillars,' he told Sandra.

So every day Sandra fed them with fresh leaves from the mulberry tree. There was never much left of yesterday's leaves, and she was amazed that such little things could eat so much. Often they grew too big for their skins, and she noticed they lost their appetites until the old skins had split and been left behind.

Several weeks later Tom came in to see them again. His eyes nearly popped out of his head! The silkworms were now about four centimetres long, and were fat and healthy. He stood still in the shed; he could hear a strange noise, like rain. But it was not raining. It was a hot, sunny day. 'What's that noise?' he asked as Grandfather came into the shed. Grandfather chuckled. 'That's the noise of all those silkworms, eating!' Tom looked at them, their heads moving to and fro as their mouths cut into the leaves. It was interesting to watch—they did not stop eating for a moment. He wished they looked a bit more colourful, though. They

120

were still grey, a paler grey now they were bigger.

A few days later Sandra was worried about some of the silkworms. 'Look, Grandfather,' she said. 'Those three over there aren't eating. They're not moving much, either. Are they ill?'

Grandfather took a careful look. The three were near the sides of the box, resting on their back stumps, with their heads and their front legs in the air, quite still. 'I think they're getting ready to start spinning their cocoons,' he told Sandra. 'They spin them from pure silk, which they make inside themselves.'

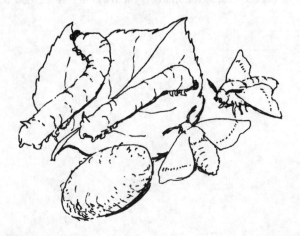

When Sandra called next day the three silkworms were busy waving their heads from side to side. She could see a soft thread of silk coming from their mouths, and noticed how they stuck it to the sides of the box as they moved round their little chosen spots. In a few days the silkworms had spun more and more, making egg-shaped cocoons round their bodies until they were invisible inside them. More of the silkworms were now spinning their cocoons, too, and Sandra marvelled at the beautiful colours of them, some a deep rich gold, others a creamy yellow.

'Tom, come and look at them now,' said Sandra, tugging him into the shed. There was no sound of eating now, and everything was still in the flat box. All round the inside the beautiful oval cocoons were fixed fast by the first threads of silk the silkworms had spun. The cocoons themselves could have been made of pure gold; they were hard and smooth, and yet velvety to touch.

'From grey to gold!' said Tom, in wonder. He was wishing he had not scoffed at the little grey worms. They had been able to make something that no man could make, pure silk, and how very beautiful it was.

Inside the cocoons the silkworms slept, and as they slept they changed: first into little bullet-shaped brown chrysalises, and then into small white moths, which bit their way through the silk to greet the world again. The mulberry leaves had gone, and the moths were very carefully laid one by one onto clean white paper in the flat box. They did not fly, or eat, but spent their days fluttering their soft creamy wings as they walked about the paper. Some laid circles of little white eggs which stuck to the paper and soon became hard and grey. Sandra and Tom knew that these little eggs were already the homes for the grey silkworms that would appear next year, just as the mulberry leaves burst from their buds.

All God's creatures

Project outline

The thought of creepy-crawlies may fill us with horror and, if it does, our squeamishness may be passed on to the children. For the more stout-hearted, however, this project will provide great interest in the class-room.

Familiar as the children are with the words 'God's world', they may view only part of it with complete admiration: the colours of flowers and butterflies, the song of birds, the majesty of fine scenery, and the variety of animal life. Beetles, spiders, worms and snails may seem to hold little fascination, but they too are part of God's world and hold an interest that can become life-long for some.

Either study one particular arthropod (the group that includes insects, spiders and crustaceans), or widen the project to find out about several different kinds. Ideas are given here.

Worms Bring in some garden soil. Show the children that it is not solid, but made up of particles which cling together or separate according to the dampness of the soil. Look at a few particles under a microscope; living organisms may be detected; or use a magnifying glass. Push a spade down into some grassy soil, so that a flat bank can be seen; worm 'burrows' may be visible. These are good to have in the garden, as they aerate it, and the worms live off decaying matter in the soil. To collect worms for close study, soak a piece of lawn with warm water which has some washing-up liquid added to it. The worms should come to the surface, and will need to be dipped immediately into a saucer of clean water or held under a running tap for a few seconds. Look at the patterns of circles on the worms and watch how they move when laid on the surface of the grass or earth. To watch them burrowing, fill a large glass bowl or sweet jar with layers of sand and soil, water well and cover with grass and dead leaves. Put the worms on this, then tie thick paper round the jar to keep out the light. Leave for three days, then take away the paper; you should be able to see how the worms have burrowed into the earth, possibly taking the dead leaves with them. Make drawings and written notes, however simple. In your games or PE activity, include 'worm movements' along with those of other creatures you study. The movements could be set to music.

Snails and slugs In very dry weather, and in winter, snails and slugs are usually hidden. They crawl into cracks in brick walls, under stones, or into old flowerpots, etc. There they stay, the snail's opening sealed with hardened mucus, until the warmer, wetter weather comes. To find slugs, put straw or dry grass cuttings round strawberry or rhubarb plants, and the slugs will shelter there during the day. Snails like to stay in brick crannies before coming out to feed. Collect a few of these creatures and put them in a glass jar or on a sheet of glass, raised so that they can be viewed from beneath to see how they move. To see snails eating, add a few pieces of damp, coloured paper to a jar and put in one or two snails. Within two days you will see thin patches on the paper, showing where the snail has scraped away part of it. The snails will leave droppings the same colour as the paper.

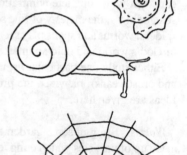

Study the spiral on the snail's shell; follow the pattern from the centre and you will find the end of the spiral is above the snail's head. Watch the movements of the head and eye-tentacles. Compare the spiral of the snail's shell with other spirals that occur in nature, on sea shells, spiders' webs, and sunflower seed-heads, etc. Make patterns from spiral shapes.

Spiders Talk about what spiders eat (smaller insects and flies). How do they catch these creatures, most of which fly? Try to find spiders' webs in the playground, and ask the children to look for them in their gardens at home. The early morning is the best time to see them, and they are particularly beautiful when covered with raindrops or dew. These webs usually have to be remade every morning. Refer back to the spiral pattern and build up a drawing of how the spider constructs each web. (Other types of spiders construct them differently and the webs are different in size and shape.) Notice how the spider lies in wait for its prey, then poisons it with a bite. Often it then wraps its prey in thread before eating it later. For a close look at a spider, keep one in a box covered with cellophane for a few days. Put in some bent wire so that the wire forms an apex, and watch the spider spin in this. Keep a small amount of damp tissue on the floor of the box so that the spider can drink from it. Release it after a few days. Count the spider's legs and compare with an ant, butterfly or bee.

Gather any materials you have to show at the Assembly, paying particular attention to the intricate detail in the creatures, and in the patterns concerned. Point out that these details are by God's design, and that nothing is too small or insignificant for his infinite care.

The Assembly

Hymns and songs

The kitten's fur is warm	NCS 11
Now the sun is shining	NCS 19
Think of a world without any flowers	SSL 15
I love God's tiny creatures	SSL 42

Poem

Look at the ant

I lay down in my garden
  to play with building bricks;
I built a sturdy castle,
  with drawbridge made of sticks.

And in the summer sunshine
  I dreamt a gleaming knight,
who rode a milk-white charger,
  came galloping in sight.

I looked again; a tiny ant
  had crossed the drawbridge stick,
and then looked up and wondered
  about the walls so thick.

It hardly hesitated
  before it scaled the wall,
it didn't need a ladder,
  or seem about to fall;

and no one heard it enter,
  so silently and smooth.
All round the castle courtyard
  the ant began to move.

My knight in shining armour
  a watchman would have seen
a long way off, and trumpets
  been sounded loud and keen.

The clip-clop of his charger
  would sound a sure alarm;
but when the ant had entered,
  the battlements stood calm.

The knight should learn a lesson
  from ants, so very small,
who silently and quickly
  would scale the castle wall.

The castle could be taken—
unlikely, though, I grant,
not by a mighty army,
but by a tiny ant!

Music

Music

Funeral March of a Marionette, Gounod
The Mouse Waltz from *Tales of Beatrix Potter,* Lanchbery
(The Gounod is a spine-chilling piece at its opening and this contrasts with the waltz, giving a very different feeling)

Prayer

O God, help us to notice the tiny creatures in your world. Help us to learn about them by watching them, so that we never destroy them carelessly or deliberately. You care for the smallest as well as the largest of your creatures, O God. Help us to care, too.

Stories

Bible stories: Four of God's creatures—Proverbs 30.24-28
     God's care in his world—Psalm 104.24-25, 27-28
Little Miss Muffet (told in full)

Little Miss Muffet

When Patience was ill, she wanted her father near. He was very good at saying the right thing to make her feel better, and he was always cheerful and made her laugh. He was also a doctor and gave her the best medicines he knew about.

Patience and Dr Thomas Muffet lived a long time ago when people were still finding out how big the world was, and what there was to see in it. Dr Muffet had discovered what fun it was to travel to other countries on the big sailing-ships, and sometimes he was away for months, calling at places Patience had never heard of, and seeing plants, people and animals that she did not know existed.

One year he went to Spain, where he found the people had learnt how to make cloth from the silk spun by a small caterpillar, a silkworm. He wrote Patience a poem about it* and sent her a little of the gold-coloured silk, so fine and yet so strong.

The King of England heard about Dr Muffet, and was interested in what he was discovering abroad, especially about insects. 'You have found out things about these small creatures that no one ever knew before,' the king wrote, and he asked to be sent a copy of the book Dr Muffet was writing about them.

Dr Muffet was pleased. He wondered if the king would be able to understand his book, though, because he was writing it in Latin and not in English. Just to make sure that the king knew it had been written especially for him, Dr Muffet wrote: 'For His Gracious Majesty, King James 1st' in it.

Back home, Dr Muffet was writing about the insects he had seen on his travels when he looked up from his window one day to watch Patience as she played in the garden. She picked some flowers, and followed a butterfly as it flitted backwards and forwards across the flower-beds. Dr Muffet sighed; he wished Patience was more interested in *all* the small creatures in the garden, like snails, ants, spiders and beetles. She liked the bright colours of the butterflies, and watched the honey-bees as they collected pollen, but she did not really like to get too close to the 'creepy-crawlies' in the garden.

Patience came indoors. 'I don't know what to do,' she said to her father.

'Why don't you go and find some caterpillars?' asked Dr Muffet hopefully.

'I'm hungry!' said Patience, and raced off to the kitchen.

A few minutes later Dr Muffet saw Patience go back into the garden with a bowl and spoon. She sat down on a tuft of grass and began to eat what looked like a rather lumpy yoghurt. She seemed to be enjoying it. Suddenly Patience leapt to her feet and dropped the bowl. She ran, crying, into the house. Dr Muffet ran to meet her.

'What's the matter?' he asked, quite alarmed.

Patience was panting and gasping, her eyes wide open. 'Father!' she cried, rushing into his arms. 'There was a big spider coming towards my skirt. I was sure it was going to crawl up the grass into my bowl of curds. It was horrible!'

Dr Muffet could not help smiling just a little. 'Patience, come with me,' he said, taking her hand. They walked over to the tuft of grass and picked up her fallen bowl. Then Dr Muffet took Patience to a nearby bush where he crouched down. 'Look at this,' he said.

Patience, still a little nervous, leant over to look. Between the leaves of the bush she could see the most beautiful silvery net, all the little strands woven into a lovely spiral pattern.

'Is it silk?' she asked, thinking of the silkworms' golden threads.

'It's a special kind of spider silk,' said her father. 'Every morning the spider spins this lovely web to catch the flies for his dinner. Usually he sits hidden in the bushes, waiting for a fly to come. I expect you brushed past the bush when you brought your bowl out here, and that disturbed the spider. But you don't need to be frightened of him; he won't hurt you.'

Dr Muffet left Patience watching the thread. He hoped she would make a picture of it later on, or embroider it in silks on a piece of cloth. He went back to his writing, but every now and again he smiled when he thought of Patience rushing indoors as the little spider came towards her. Instead of getting on with the book he was writing, he took up his pen and wrote:

> Little Miss Muffet
> sat on a tuffet,
> eating her curds and whey.

There came a big spider,
and sat down beside her,
and frightened Miss Muffet away.

* *The Silk Worme and its Flies*

(This story is fabricated from the common belief that the nursery rhyme originated during the reign of King James I of England when a Dr Muffet was making a study of insects and spiders, a subject about which little was known at the time. Adapted from information in *Origins of Rhymes, Songs and Sayings* by Jean Harrowven, Kaye and Ward, 1982.)